THE CUSTOMS AND EXCISE SERVICE IN FINGAL

1684–1765

Sober, Active and Bred to the Sea

Maynooth Studies in Local History

GENERAL EDITOR Raymond Gillespie

This pamphlet is one of eight new additions to the Maynooth Studies in Local History series in 1999. Like their twenty predecessors, most are based on theses submitted for the M.A. in Local History at National University of Ireland, Maynooth. The pamphlets are not concerned primarily with the portrayal of the history of 'particular places'. All are local in their focus but that localisation is determined not by administrative boundaries but rather the limits of the experience of everyday life in the regions of Ireland over time. In some of these works the local experience is of a single individual while in others social, occupational or religious groups form the primary focus of enquiry.

The results of these enquiries into the shaping of local societies in the past emphasises, again, the diversity of the Irish historical experience. Ranging across problems of economic disaster, political transformation, rural unrest and religious tension, these works show how such problems were grounded in the realities of everyday life in local communities. The responses to such challenges varied from region to region, each place coping with problems in its own way, determined by its historical evolution and contemporary constraints.

The result of such investigations can only increase our awareness of the complexity of Ireland's historical evolution. Each work, in its own right, is also a significant contribution to our understanding of how specific Irish communities have developed in all their richness and diversity. In all, they demonstrate the vibrancy and challenging nature of local history.

Maynooth Studies in Local History: Number 28

THE CUSTOMS AND EXCISE SERVICE IN FINGAL 1684–1765

Sober, Active and Bred to the Sea

Maighréad Ní Mhurchadha

IRISH ACADEMIC PRESS
DUBLIN • PORTLAND, OR

First published in 1999 by
IRISH ACADEMIC PRESS
44, Northumberland Road, Dublin 4, Ireland
and in the United States of America by
IRISH ACADEMIC PRESS
c/o ISBS, 5804 NE Hassalo Street, Portland, OR 97213.

website: www.iap.ie

British Library Cataloguing in Publication Data
Mhurchadha, Maighread Ni
The Customs and Excise Service in Fingal, 1684–1785: Sober, Active and Bred to the sea. – (Maynooth studies in local history; 28)
1. Smuggling – Ireland – Fingal – History 2. Customs administration – Ireland – History 3. Customs administration – Ireland – Fingal – Officials and employees – History
I. Title
364. 1'33'0941835
ISBN 0716526727

Library of Congress Cataloging-in-Publication Data
Ní Mhurchadha, Maighréad.
The Customs and Excise Service in Fingal, 1684–1785: Sober, Achive and Bred to the sea/Maighréad Ní Mhurchadha.
p. cm. — (Maynooth studies in local history: No. 28.)
Includes bibliographical references (p.) and index.
ISBN 0–7165–2672–7 (pkb.)
1. Customs administration—Ireland—Fingal (County)—History. 2. Smuggling—Ireland—Fingal (County)—History. 3. Fingal (Dublin, Ireland: County)—History. I. Title. II. Series.
HJ6899. F56N5 1999
352.4'48'094183—dc21
99–29352
CIP

Typeset in 10 pt on 12 pt Bembo by
Carrigboy Typesetting Services, County Cork
Printed by ColourBooks Ltd, Dublin

Contents

FIGURES

Acknowledgements

I should like to express my thanks to all who assisted me in the course of the research for this study especially the staffs of Dublin City Archives, Fingal Heritage Centre, Swords, Gilbert Library, Dublin, Gloucestershire County Council Record Office, Grand Lodge of the A. F. & A. Masons of Ireland, National Library of Ireland, Public Record Office, Kew, Representative Church Body Library, Dublin, Trinity College Dublin Library and University College Dublin (Folklore Department); Rev. Ronald Watts, Rector, Holmpatrick, for permission to photograph the Weston tablet and Jack Benton, Balbriggan, who photographed it; Maree Baker, Peadar Bates, Jim Walsh and all my friends in the Balbriggan and District, Donabate, Loughshinny and Rush and Skerries Historical Societies for information and encouragement; the staff of the Department of Modern History, Maynooth College, my fellow-students in the MA Local History course of 1996–98 and the course directors, Dr. Mary Ann Lyons and Dr. Raymond Gillespie, supervisor for this study, for their help and guidance.

TECHNICAL NOTES

Dates

Dates in the text, up to and including 2 September 1752, are old style, but with the year starting on 1 January.

Spelling and punctuation

Spelling, including the spelling of place-names, and punctuation have been modernised in quotations.

Introduction

The purpose of this study is to tell the story of one community and its relationships to other overlapping communities. Alan Rogers defines local history as 'the study of the past of some significant local unit, developing as a community, in its context and compared with other such units'. He goes on to say:

> The subject chosen may be a village or it may be some other unit, such as an estate or a firm. Any association of men, whether undertaken voluntarily or compulsorily, with common interests, concerns the historian, and where these fall below the national level, they are properly the concern of the local historian.[1]

Raymond Gillespie and Gerard Moran write that 'our understanding of the history of the dynamics of the many overlapping communities within the different regions of Ireland remains sketchy'.[2]

This study (a shortened version of the author's MA thesis) is concerned with the lives and careers of the men who were assigned specifically to stations in the customs and excise service in Fingal during the period 1684 to 1765. Fingal is defined as the traditional area of Fingal, that is, that part of north County Dublin situated between the rivers Tolka and Delvin. It thus includes several areas, such as Finglas, Drumcondra, Fairview and Clontarf which are now part of Dublin city. No part of Fingal is more than eleven miles from the coast.

During the late seventeenth and early eighteenth centuries the area was essentially rural and had no large towns. The coastal region was mainly flat and was noted then, as it is today, for its fertility. A short distance inland there were low hills. Several small off-shore islands presented hazards to shipping and provided havens for smugglers. The most important features of the area, from the point of view of this study, were the two estuaries, the Rogerstown Estuary between Rush and Portrane and the Broadmeadow Estuary between Donabate and Malahide. Before the building of the railway in the nineteenth century, these estuaries provided access for small boats almost as far as the main road, that is, the turnpike road leading to Dublin through Swords or to the north through Balrothery. The customs service, therefore, had to guard a long expanse of coast as well as several small creeks and harbours.

The oldest surviving set of comprehensive personnel records for the Irish customs and excise service dates from 1684 while 1765 was the date of the coming into operation of the Revestment Act, which provided for the purchase of the fiscal rights of the Isle of Man by the British crown. The Revestment Act marked a watershed in the history of smuggling and this had an important bearing on the work of the customs and excise, particularly in Fingal.

The main sources used for the study are the revenue records (establishment or salary books and minutes of the revenue commissioners) held at the Public Records Office at Kew, contemporary newspapers and church records. The revenue commissioners were concerned with general administration, with personnel matters, with the building and maintenance of ships, watch-houses and other revenue property and with difficulties and disputes. Seizures, which were regarded as one of the principal measures of success in the eighteenth century, were seldom discussed unless they caused problems or required special action. Since the seizure books, which were kept as a matter of routine, have not, as far as is known, survived, it is necessary to rely on the newspaper accounts for information about the success stories of the customs and excise officers.

The first section of this work will examine the development of the customs and excise service as a whole in Fingal during the period 1684 to 1765. Secondly, we will look at the working lives of the individual officers. The third part will investigate, insofar as it is possible, the personal lives of the revenue officers, their families and their relationships with their churches and the wider community.

1. The Custom House, Essex Quay, *c.*1753, headquarters of the revenue commissioners, the Port of Dublin customs district and the County Dublin excise district (*Courtesy National Library of Ireland*)

The development of the service in Fingal, 1684–1765

When Charles II returned to England in 1660 he found he had serious financial problems to deal with. In 1662 the Irish parliament set out to solve these, insofar as they affected this country, by passing two acts, the Act of Tonnage and Poundage (better known as the Customs Act) and the Act of Excise.[1] Customs was an old levy which could be charged on either exports or imports. The 1662 Act was designed to update and regularise the system as well as to bring in more revenue. Excise, on the other hand, was described in the title of the act as 'the excise or new impost'. This form of taxation, which had been introduced to Ireland in the seventeenth century, imposed a duty of 'inland excise' on ale, beer and strong waters as well as a duty of 'import excise' on most imported goods.

The management of the revenue was assigned to not more than seven and not less than five customs commissioners.[2] An office of excise was set up in Dublin and was to be managed by not more than five commissioners and a surveyor.[3] In practice, five of the customs commissioners acted as excise commissioners and the whole body was generally known under the title of 'revenue commissioners' or 'board of revenue'.

Little is known about the organisation of the revenue service at local level before 1684. The customs service was divided into districts, each district consisting of a major port together with certain other creeks and harbours in the neighbourhood. The districts were, in turn, subdivided into 'rides' or 'ridings'. The excise service was also divided into districts, each headed by a collector and manned by a number of gaugers. Each full gauger was assigned to a 'walk'. The structure of both services was hierarchical and was as tightly controlled and disciplined as conditions would allow. As the excise service developed the government not only acquired a countrywide agency for the collection of revenue but also an efficient network for the gathering and dissemination of information. This was particularly important at a time when travel was slow and difficult.

In 1968 L.M. Cullen discussed the emergence of entrepôt centres, situated 'as far as possible from the main provisioning ports . . . and as close as possible to the ultimate market . . . ' in the smuggling business.[4] He continued as follows:

> Fishing vessels were ideal for ferrying goods from the entrepôt to their final destination. Wherries – vessels of up to 15 or 20 tons – used in the coastal fisheries became the main means of conveyance of smuggled

goods on the east coast of Ireland. Rush, a busy fishing port in north county Dublin, close to the main Irish centre of consumption of dutiable goods, became the home base for a large fleet of wherries, for which fishing was a purely marginal or a cover activity. Rush's rise to prominence in the running trade was, however, not due solely to its fishing or adjacency to the Dublin market. It eventuated also from its convenient situation for vessels sailing from the Isle of Man, which established itself at an early stage as the entrepôt base of the smuggling trade. Indeed, as soon as the Peace of Utrecht had brought to an end the war-time interruption of trade, business with the island, small in the late seventeenth century, began to expand rapidly. The rise of Rush's smuggling trade was in large measure a function of the flourishing of the Isle of Man as an entrepôt centre.

Figure 2 shows the location of the Fingal customs and excise stations. Throughout most of the period covered by this study the excise service in Fingal was technically part of the County Dublin excise. The first formal assignment to a Fingal walk was made in the second quarter of 1695 when Edward Giles was assigned to Finglas, a village situated on one of the main roads leading north.[5] A year later Joshua Beale was assigned to Swords and Edward Moone to Corduff, near the village of Lusk.[6] No further walks were established

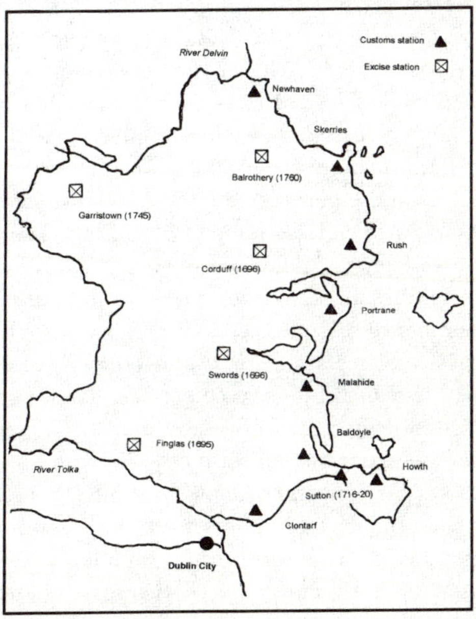

2. Customs and excise stations in Fingal, 1684–1765 (incl.)

in Fingal until 1745 when William Sherriff was appointed to Garristown in the north-west of the area.[7] North-east Fingal had to wait until late 1760 for its first formal assignment of an excise officer, when John Revell was appointed to Balrothery. At the same time Matthew Dowling was confirmed and continued as surveyor of the North Survey, in which capacity he had apparently been serving informally. The appointment of Robert Shaw as supernumerary gauger, that is, a junior gauger who would be available to provide cover in any walk in the area in the event of the absence of the permanent gauger, to the North Survey in 1763 completed the slow development of the North Survey as a self-contained excise area within the Dublin County district.[8]

As far as the administration of the customs service was concerned, the Fingal coast, together with the creeks in south County Dublin and Bray, formed part of the Port of Dublin district throughout the period 1684–1765. In a detailed countrywide report on the service written for the revenue commissioners in 1675 Timothy Whiteinge referred to an earlier account which he had sent to the commissioners on conditions in Fingal. In January 1675 he had reported on visits to Clontarf, Howth, Baldoyle, Malahide, Rush and Skerries while in April 1675 he visited the same stations, with the exception of Baldoyle, but including Portrane.[9] As far as is known the earlier account covering the Fingal harbours has not survived. Since seven stations were inspected there must have been at least seven customs officers serving in Fingal at the time. Newhaven, situated about a mile north of the present town of Balbriggan, is not mentioned in Whiteinge's report but by 1684 it was clearly a separate station.

In 1684 the customs service had eleven employees based in Fingal.[10] Baldoyle, Howth, Malahide, Newhaven, Portrane and Rush had one waiter (coast officer) each while Clontarf had two. Skerries had a surveyor and two watermen (boatmen). As can be seen from Figure 3, based on an analysis of establishments data, the numbers in the customs service increased fairly steadily during most of the period 1684–1765 but rose steeply in the 1760s. If, however, the land-based and sea-going staff are charted separately a different picture emerges. (See Figure 4.) The increase in the number of land-based staff was modest given the increase in external trade during the period.[11] The increase in the number of sea-going coxons and boatmen, however, can only be described as spectacular, particularly towards the end of the period. Figure 5 shows the extent to which the balance between land-based and sea-going staff had changed, both in absolute and relative terms, between 1684 and 1765.

The growth in the sea-going part of the service can only be explained in terms of the fight against smuggling. Land-based officers, including surveyors, land-waiters (or coast officers) and tide-waiters, were required to implement the ordinary provisions of the legislation, for example, the collection of duties, the routine rummaging of ships, the discharge of cargoes inwards and outwards, the protection of wrecks. Barges were needed to intercept the smugglers at sea before they had an opportunity to land run goods.

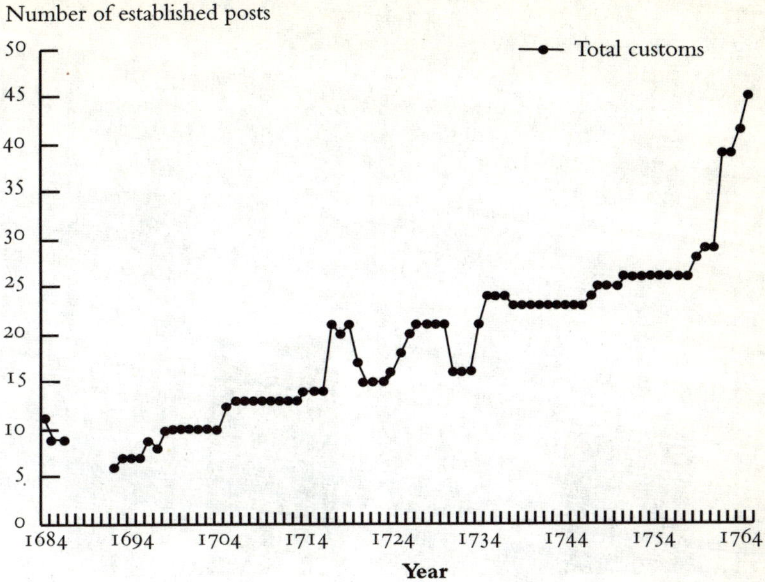

3. Fingal area – customs employees 1684–1765

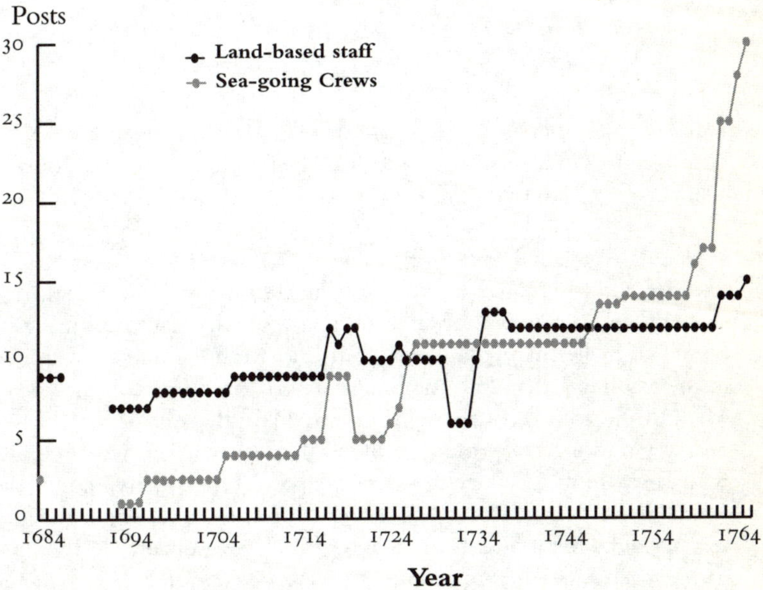

4. Fingal area – land-based and sea-going customs staff 1684–1765

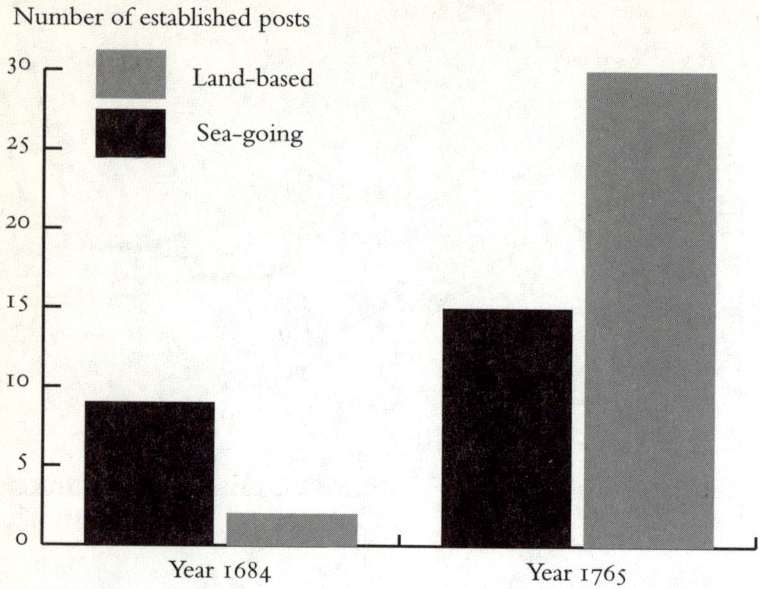

5. Fingal area – customs employees 1684 and 1765

This change in emphasis was the result of a deliberate change in policy on the commissioners' part. It was articulated in a stern rebuke of the commissioners of 27 January 1738 as follows:

> Write to Mr. Boyd, surveyor at Malahide, Mr. Weston, surveyor at Skerries, and Mr. Howell, surveyor at Queensborough [near Drogheda], that the commissioners observe by many small seizures returned to them and by frequent complaints of rescues from the officers stationed in their country, that a clandestine trade is carried on with the Isle of Man, to the scandal of the said surveyors and the rest of the officers properly stationed to prevent it, and as the surveyors are well supplied with every thing necessary to secure and protect his majesty's duties, the board are fully convinced this evil arises from the surveyors' negligence and inactivity for, if their boats kept to sea in all reasonable weather, and had a sharp look out when they expected boats returning from the island, this mischief might be prevented, for though the officers may not be strong enough to seize on shore, when the country come in to the

> runners assistance, yet if they met them at sea, the surveyors and their hands would be more than sufficient to give a good account of them. They are not to imagine their boats and hands are kept only for boarding ships when they anchor in their roads. Were it so, arms and ammunition were needless and their instructions, if regarded, would inform them, that the said surveyors and their hands are stationed to prevent the running trade. The board expect a speedy regulation in their conduct for the future, by a more vigorous behaviour, by keeping a constant correspondence &c. and acting in concert, one with the other, by constantly going to sea and by using all legal means to prevent the landing goods. A practice of this kind may restore them to the favour of the board, otherwise the commissioners will think themselves under a necessity of placing more diligent officers in their room, or of totally suppressing their boats and hands; the board being determined never to support such an expense without the least colour of advantage to the public.[12]

The two Fingal officers in Skerries and Malahide, who were so severely reprimanded, were neither particularly senior nor were they highly-paid. At the time George Weston of Skerries enjoyed a salary of £40 a year while George Boyd's annual salary as surveyor of Malahide amounted to £35.[13] By contrast, the salary of a revenue commissioner was £1,000.

Customs employees could enter the service by various routes. One entry grade was that of waterman (later boatman). Boatmen had the prospect of promotion to coxon. The grade of tide-waiter did not exist, at least officially, in Fingal until late in the period.

The basic entry grade for customs officers in Fingal was waiter, later called coast officer. To a large extent the coast officer combined the duties of riding officer, land-waiter and tide-waiter. Promotion was to the grade of surveyor. While there was only one surveyor (at Skerries) in 1684 by 1765 there were three, at Baldoyle, Malahide and Skerries, as well as the more senior post of riding surveyor, to which young customs officers might aspire.[14] By 1765 there were two posts of deputy surveyor, one at Skerries and the other at Malahide. However, the salary of a deputy surveyor was lower than that of a coast officer.

The entry grade for the excise service was supernumerary gauger. Officers were promoted, usually in order of seniority by province, to full gauger. For most of the period under review this was the most senior excise post in Fingal and officers who aspired to promotion had to leave the area. In 1760 the post of surveyor of the North Survey was created when Mathew Dowling was appointed, thus providing local officers with at least the remote prospect of promotion locally.

While both customs and excise employees were liable to be transferred to any part of the country it was unusual for an officer to move between one service and the other. There were exceptions, however. George Steer was the County Dublin

Table 1. Salaries paid to customs and excise officers in selected years, in the period 1684–1764 (incl.)

Grade	*Year*								
	1684	1694	1704	1714	1724	1734	1744	1754	1764
Customs/land-based	£	£	£	£	£	£	£	£	£
Riding surveyor	–	–	–	–	65	65	65	65	65
Surveyor	40	–	40	40	40	40	40	50	50
Deputy surveyor	–	–	–	–	–	–	–	–	30
Coast officer/waiter	30/35	35	35/40	35/40	35/40	35/40	35/40	35	35
Tidewaiter	–	–	–	–	–	–	–	30	30
Customs/Sea-going									
Coxon	–	–	–	–	16	16	16/20	20/21	23
Boatman/waterman	20	20	10	15	15	15	15	15/20	20
Excise									
Surveyor	–	–	–	–	–	–	–	–	65
Gauger	–	–	40	40	40	40	40	40	40
Supernumerary gauger	–	–	–	–	–	–	–	–	30

Source: P. R. O., CUST 20

supernumerary gauger in the excise service stationed at Skerries. Described by the surveyor, George Weston, as 'bred to the sea, . . . sober, active, resolute, and well accustomed to making seizures', Steer was appointed in 1760 to succeed George Wahab as tide-waiter.[15] It is clear from this and other references that ability as a sailor was considered essential for success as a customs officer.

Salaries did not change greatly during the period. Table 1 shows the annual salaries paid to the various grades represented in Fingal in selected years. Boatmen were originally paid £20 per annum. When John Daly departed from Skerries in 1695 his successors, Michael Daly and Michael Dennis, were paid £12 and £8 respectively.[16] In 1702, the two Skerries boatmen, William Bishop and Michael Dennis, were paid £10 apiece.[17] The salaries of the four Skerries boatmen were raised to £12 in 1706 and to £15 in 1709.[18] They remained at that until 1746 when, following a joint petition by the surveyor and boatmen, they were raised to £20 per annum although the salaries of the boatmen in Rush and Malahide remained at the lower level.[19] The petition throws considerable light on the economic circumstances of the boatmen as well as on the unexpected consequences of certain political decisions. The petition stated, concerning the boatmen:

> That they labour under great losses by the late act of parliament for burning boats seized with run goods; that for several years past the said boatmen's moiety of seizures made in the barge amounted to between thirty and forty pounds per annum, which enabled them to keep the sea very constantly; and since the commencement of the said act they have

> been as much at sea, as before, but not with the like success, having seized only one boat by accident which was burnt pursuant to the directions in the said statute; that they have chased several boats which had very considerable quantities of goods on board to be run, to the great hazard of their lives, which the people threw over board to save their boats, and which by very good informations amounted to the value of sixteen hundred pounds and upwards, which is a great discouragement to the petitioners after having been 10 or 12 nights successively at sea in the worst of weather and depth of winter, to reap no benefit for their great fatigue and labour; that they are cruising at sea at least two-thirds of the year, which, since the said act commenced, has exhausted what little substance the boatmen had saved before by seizures, in providing provisions for themselves on their said cruises and maintaining their wives and children at home; that all the seizures they now can make is at land where the expenses to informers, horse hire and other incident charges run away with the greatest part of the profit; that they have near 200 ships that annually put into the road of Skerries, which the petitioners are obliged to board in all weathers without any sort of perquisite whatever; that the seizures made by the petitioners heretofore are more considerable than any other barge has done in the kingdom for many years, and by the particular diligence and activity of the surveyor, Mr. Weston, the smugglers in Fingal (a most notorious band) have met with greater checks and been more distressed than they ever were by any of his predecessors, which may fully appear by the many considerable seizures made by him and his means, entered in the several information books in this port; that his salary at present is only £40 a year, which is £10 less than most other tide surveyors in Ireland, and his boatmen have but £15 per annum, which is £5 less than many other boatmen whose duty is by no means so severe and constant as the petitioners.

The commissioners accepted these arguments and granted the salary increases. The boatmen at Malahide had to wait until 1759 and the single boatman at Rush until 1763 for similar increases.[20]

Revenue officers concerned to supplement their salaries were restricted in the types of business they were permitted to carry on. The legislation laid down the following rules:

> No commissioner, comptroller, customer, or any other officer of the customs, their deputies or servants, shall have any ship of their own, or shall buy or sell by way of merchandise, or shall meddle with freighting or shipping, or have or occupy any wharf or quay, or hold any hostelry or tavern, or shall be any factor or attorney for any merchant, or shall be host to any merchant, or shall be a common officer, or deputy of any

> common officers in the city, town borough, or town where he or they shall be collector, comptroller or searcher, upon pain of losing his or their office or employments as to the customs.[21]

The officers of the revenue had to find other ways of supplementing their income. The petition of the Skerries boatmen already quoted makes it clear that they were greatly dependent on the money earned through seizures. It was customary to sell the produce of seizures 'by the candle' (by public auction) and, after any expenses had been deducted, to divide the proceeds equally into the 'king's moiety' and the 'informer's moiety'. The informer's moiety was divided according to a pre-determined arrangement among any of those who had been involved in the seizure either by providing information leading to the seizure or by actually making the seizure. Tables 2 and 3 show the distribution of two such 'informer's moieties' (£188 and £26), resulting from seizures which had been made on 8 April 1731 at Lambay and on 1 August 1731 at Ireland's Eye.[22]

Table 2. Distribution of a moiety of a seizure – 18 May 1731

	£	s	d
To Mr Howell, surveyor of Skerries	30	–	–
To Robert Watson, boatman	25	–	–
To Robert Westicoat, boatman	25	–	–
To Alexander Tomkins, coast officer	21	12	–
To Richard Sankey, boatman at Rush	21	12	–
To John Willett, boatman at Skerries	21	12	–
To Peter Druly, boatman at Skerries	21	12	–
To George Wahab, boatman at Skerries	21	12	–
TOTAL	188	–	–

Source: P.R.O., CUST 1/23, 18 May 1731

Table 3. Distribution of a moiety of a seizure – 3 November 1731

		£	s	d
To Mr Howell, surveyor of Skerries		6	10	–
To Joshua Wahab, tide-water		6	10	–
To Peter Druly	Boatmen	3	5	–
To Robert Westicoat	Boatmen	3	5	–
To Thomas Evans	Boatmen	3	5	–
To John Willett	Boatmen	3	5	–
TOTAL		26	–	–

Source: P.R.O., CUST 1/23, 3 November 1731

This scanty evidence shows that seizures could vary in value but it also shows that boatmen, in particular, could earn considerably more than their annual salaries through the produce of one valuable seizure. It is not surprising, therefore, that the Skerries boatmen were appalled by the decision of parliament in 1743 to burn any boats seized for running goods.[23] Ironically, they had made the first seizure of a suitable boat for burning, on which occasion the commissioners directed

> Mr. Fowke, the collector, and Mr. Burleigh, inspector general of the customs, to attend at Ringsend next Wednesday being the 1st August and take care that she be effectively burnt with all her tackle &c., pursuant to a late act of parliament and they are to give a barrel of ale to the persons who attend the burning of her and the board will allow them the expense.[24]

By 1745 parliament recognised the difficulty of motivating the officers and offered a reward not exceeding £15 to any person or persons who seized a boat or wherry employed in the running of goods.[25] In 1747 the law was again amended to provide for the taking over of seized boats by the revenue as an alternative to burning.[26] Two years later an act was passed which, having stated explicitly that 'it is apprehended that the burning of such boats or wherries hath greatly discouraged the officers of his majesty's revenue from seizing such boats or wherries, and the goods, wares and merchandises run or intended to be run in them', reverted to the system of sale by auction and division into two moieties for boats as well as other goods.[27]

Other types of incentives were used to try to combat smuggling. On appointment each officer was granted a commission which enabled him to carry out his duties under the law. These included the making of seizures. From time to time the commissioners found it necessary to empower others, such as naval and army officers who were called in to aid the revenue, to make seizures by granting them commissions. Supernumerary officers, such as the tide-waiter, William Walker, and the boatmen, Richard Byers and Alexander Dugall of Malahide, were granted commissions in 1745 'to authorise and protect them in making seizures' after the commissioners had assured themselves that they were Protestants.[28]

Commissions were also granted to individuals, known as 'preventive officers' or 'waiting officers' to enable them to assist the revenue by making seizures. The commissioners' minutes of 22 August 1745 provide information both on the appointment procedures and methods of payment of these officers:

> George Weston, surveyor at Skerries and George Boyd, coast surveyor in Fingal, their report dated the 13th inst., on the petition of David Byas, deputy portreeve of Swords, setting forth that he was very active and resolute in the affair when Mr. Jolly [surveyor of Malahide] was murdered and defended him to the utmost of his power, that they are of opinion

> he is a very proper person to be employed in the king's service and granting him a commission with some small allowance they are of opinion will be of great advantage to the revenue; such a person being very necessary to be stationed at Swords.
>
> On consideration of the said affair, ordered that the said David Byas have a commission accordingly and be allowed £5 per annum to be paid quarterly out of the incidents, by the collector of Dublin Port, to commence from Michaelmas next; and also £20 per annum out of the king's moiety of such seizures as he shall make, or shall be made by his means.[29]

Morgan Carrick of Clontarf was commissioned as a waiting officer at his own request in April 1750. A marginal note in the minute book, which reads 'appointed a preventing officer at Clontarf' seems to confirm that the titles 'waiting officer' and 'preventive officer' were interchangeable.[30] The frequency with which the preventive officers' names appeared in both the commissioners' minutes and in newspapers in connection with seizures suggests that they found the revenue service a satisfying and lucrative profession. One also has the impression that they had both the freedom and flexibility to bridge the gap between the customs and excise services.

Now and then we find references to private informers in the minutes but names are seldom mentioned. A dispute between two coast officers, Thomas Brown of Newhaven, and John Walker of Mornington (near Drogheda) in 1725 was referred to the collector of Drogheda for adjudication. The commissioners said:

> They thought it proper to acquaint him, that the informer (who desires his name may be concealed) has made affidavit that on or about the 22 of July last he called Thomas Brown out of bed, and desired him and his sons to go along the lands of Ballymad [a townland south of present-day Balbriggan] and they would find a parcel of horses laden with leaf tobacco, and accordingly the said sons of Mr. Brown did find the said tobacco, and what the said Mr. Brown's sons seized was not in Balrothery Chapel when they made the seizure.[31]

In 1738 the commissioners sought to regularise the position of private informers and to devise a fair system for payment of the 'informer's moiety'.[32] Provided he fulfilled certain conditions the private informer was to receive one-third of the net produce of the moiety, the officer who received the information was to be allowed a third and the remainder was to be divided equally between the officers and other persons who made the seizure. It is clear that private informers were held in high regard by the authorities.

As well as competent seamen the revenue needed safe and secure harbours for their increasing numbers of boats. The officers, established and unestablished, had to operate in a difficult environment for much of the period under review. Fingal, and more particularly Rush and its surrounding area, were a hot-bed of smuggling. A perceptive contemporary observer, Isaac Butler, described Rush on 16 July 1744 as follows:

> Near the latter [Rush] there is a vast tract of land under rabbit burrows. This town is near an English mile in length [and] lies upon a sandy bank. Most of the houses are built of mud and covered with straw and exceedingly well peopled. By a modest computation 'tis said there is between 300/400 souls. The men are all employed in the fishing and smuggling trade. A melancholy instance thereof happened the very time I came there. The officers had made a seizure of brandy, tobacco, teas and canary wine to the amount of upwards of 250 l. sterling which they drove on carts to Dublin. Early the next morning it was partly hidden in land behind their houses. The quay lies eastward below the town, which is in [the] form of an L. The entrance is very dangerous from S. E. and by E. between two ledges of rocks on the port and larboard side. What is very particular is that the rocks on one side are all flat to the horizon, whereas those on the other are perpendicular.[33]

Scalé and Richards, in their book of maps published in 1765 which was used extensively by the revenue commissioners, stated that Rush Harbour admitted only small craft and that the passage was very narrow (Figure 6).[34] This may partly explain why the smugglers there were so successful. Their wherries were purpose-built to enter a difficult harbour like Rush whereas the large revenue barges, on the whole, were designed for combat in the open sea.

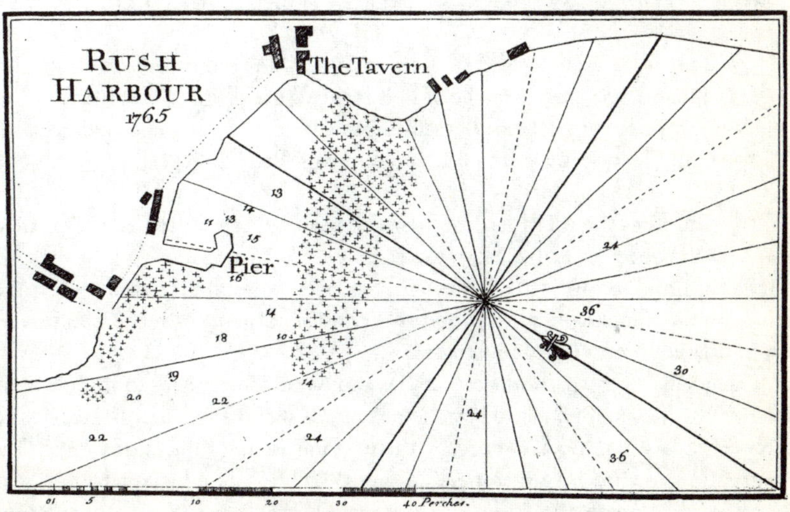

6. Rush Harbour, 1765, Scalé and Richards

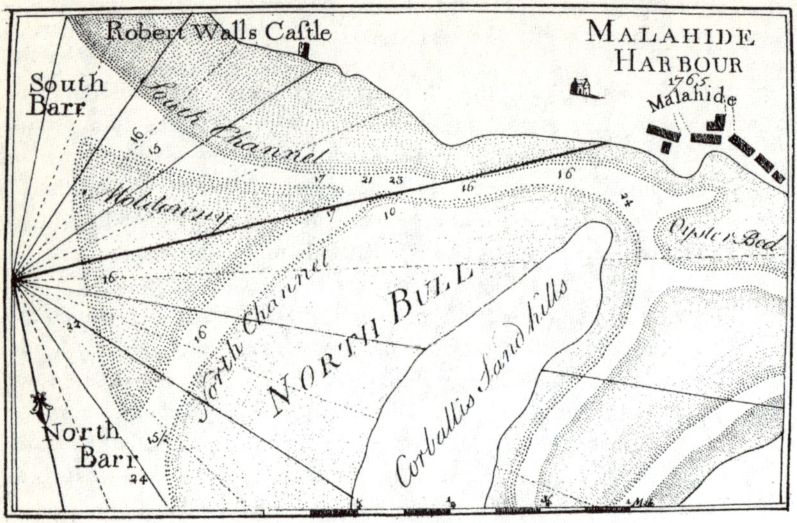

7. Malahide Harbour, 1765, Scalé and Richards

Isaac Butler described the channel to Malahide as 'very deep and large' and went on to say that it would 'admit ships of a large burden at high water as far as the town of Malahide'.[35] Scalé and Richards described the channel as a 'good harbour' but warned of the dangers of the Moldowny sandbank in the mouth of the channel (Figure 7).[36]

Skerries Harbour was generally held in high regard. Isaac Butler stated:

> The quay is situated under a peninsula of high land pistol shot from the mainland, which covers the vessels from east and south-east storms. The entrance is very safe and commodious being free from all danger and having deep water a small distance from shore.[37]

Shortly after that the memorial of the Skerries boatmen estimated that nearly 200 vessels were entering Skerries each year.[38] Later, in 1765, Scalé and Richards pointed out that, although Skerries was chiefly frequented by fishing-boats and small crafts, sometimes the packets and other vessels put in when unable to enter Dublin (Figure 8).[39]

The quality of the harbours at Skerries and Malahide explains to some extent at least why they were favoured by the revenue as stations for their barges. These barges and the other boats owned by the revenue are the subject of a great deal of attention in the commissioners' minutes. They were reluctant to delegate functions relating to the boats, with the result that a wealth of information

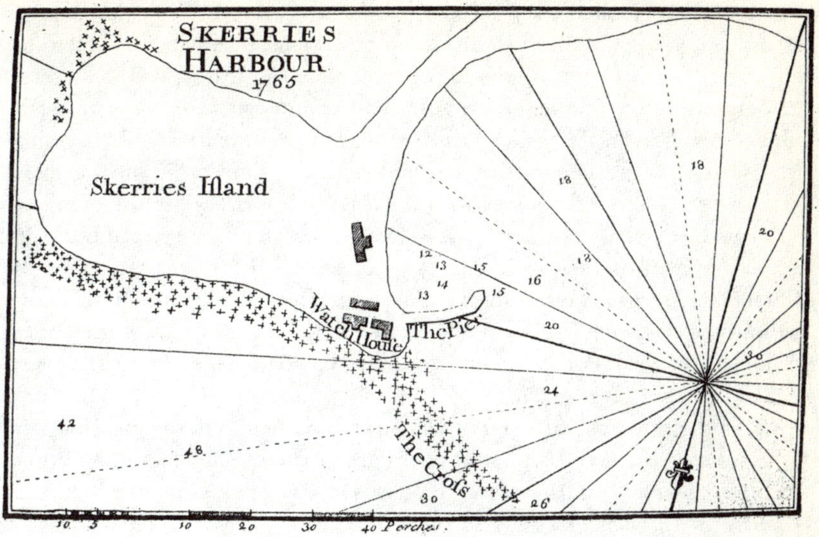

8. Skerries Harbour, 1765, Scalé and Richards

survives concerning these vessels. Boats were stationed at Skerries throughout the period and at Malahide from 1723.[40] Clontarf had a barge from 1716 to 1719.[41] Portrane was the original choice as the location for a third barge in March 1761, 'where she must be the greatest check on the smugglers, particularly at Rush and Lambay'.[42] Following unsuccessful attempts to find accommodation in Portrane for the surveyor and crew the commissioners decided to relocate them at Baldoyle where there was 'a good harbour and a place of safety for the boat'.[43]

The commissioners' reluctance to delegate purchasing powers relating to the barges gave rise to tensions between local officers who wished to have boats repaired quickly and to purchase supplies locally and the commissioners who insisted for a long time that all repairs to revenue boats should be carried out under the supervision of the revenue surveyors at Ringsend and who tried to operate a primitive system of central purchasing in relation to items such as candles, rigging and sail-cloth. Slowly and gradually the balance tilted towards the local areas, reflecting as much as anything else the development of trades and small industries associated with the sea and shipping in Skerries and Malahide. By 1765 the revenue had three large barges (at Baldoyle, Malahide and Skerries) and several small craft. From the 1730s, at least, these vessels were armed.

Although a few violent incidents had taken place there is little evidence of serious armed conflict between officers and smugglers in Fingal before 1731 when Richard Sankey was assaulted on the quay at Rush.[44] In 1735 it was reported that Samuel Jolly, surveyor at Malahide was to be delivered thirteen guns or muskets, two blunderbusses and two hangers (short swords) 'bought by him at the last cant at the Custom House for use of the Malahide barge'.[45] Later the same year, when it was reported that the Skerries barge had only two blunderbusses, four muskets were provided.[46] From this time on arms were supplied regularly to the barges. Carbines with bayonets, cartridge boxes with belts, cutlasses, pistols, gunpowder, lead, flints and swan shot are among the items listed. In 1741 William Goodeffe, boatman at Rush was allowed a case of pistols and a cutlass.[47] In 1747 Richard Shaw of Howth and Thomas Turner of Baldoyle were each provided 'with one carbine of about 2 ft. 6 inches long, a case of pistols of about 6 inches in the barrel and a good hanger'.[48] Small arms and ammunition 'without which they [the crew] cannot go on duty' were provided at the outset for the new barge at Portrane (later transferred to Baldoyle) in 1761.[49] By then arms had become an essential part of a barge's equipment.

While the principal activities of the customs service were the collection of duties on imports and the pursuit of defaulters the officers had some other functions. The customs service was responsible for collecting duties on exports as well as on imports.

Embargoes on food, particularly on corn, exports were occasionally imposed either in periods of famine and scarcity or in time of war.[50] The implementation of quarantine regulations was an important duty of the customs service but as there were no quarantine stations in the area the Fingal officers did not have any exceptional duties during periods of quarantine. While seizures of exports and the strict implementation of quarantine regulations may have been a source of irritation to many people, one public service, the care of stranded vessels and wrecks by the customs officers, was generally appreciated at least by the merchants and local gentry.

A rare tribute, paid to the customs service on 14 December 1759, was reported in the press as follows:

> At a meeting of the merchants and traders concerned in the cargo of the *Duke of Bedford* sloop from Chester ... it was agreed their thanks should be publicly given to George Weston, esq., surveyor of Skerries, and his officers, for their care and vigilance in preserving the cargo from being pillaged, when she had ran foul of an anchor there.[51]

The customs and excise service in Fingal, originally set up to collect duties on behalf of the crown, found itself increasingly involved in the fight against smuggling. This is reflected in the huge expansion of the service, particularly as regards the number of boatmen and armed vessels. Such a level of extra resources would not have been necessary to cope with the undoubted rise in the volume of legitimate trade. The experiences of individual officers in this increasingly busy and violent milieu will be considered in the next section.

Working for the Service

How did the individual officer respond to the challenge of working in the customs and excise service? How did he cope with the day-to-day routines? What difficulties did he encounter? These are some of the questions which it is hoped to answer in this section.

Many of the practices relating to appointment and training were clearly in place before 1696, the date of the earliest surviving minute book. It is, however, possible to deduce some of these from later sources, particularly when changes in the regulations took place, but others, such as a minimum or maximum age at entry (except in the case of boatmen) or a minimum standard of education, are not known. One thing is clear, however. An officer had to be prepared to subscribe to the oath of supremacy and the oath of allegiance.[1] In December 1740 the commissioners ordered that

> no person have an order of instructions in any branch of the revenue, or be admitted to be otherwise employed therein, until a certificate is produced signed by the minister, or curate and church wardens of the parish where such person was born signifying that such person was born of Protestant parents, or at least that he has been bred up as a Protestant from his infancy, and has to the best of their knowledge continued a Protestant ever since, or in case such person being bred a Papist and has renounced that religion in proper form, that a certificate to that purpose be produced from the minister or curate and church wardens of the parish, where such recantation was made.[2]

The rules excluding Catholics were strictly enforced. Randall (later Sir Randall) O'Neill, appointed as coast officer in Rush in 1749, had conformed in St. Michan's parish in Dublin, shortly before his first posting to Ballyshannon in 1747.[3] Daniel Byrne, a Malahide boatman was dismissed for being a Catholic in 1741.[4] Three other boatmen at Malahide were dismissed in 1762 for reasons which included either being a Catholic or being married to a Catholic.[5]

Other qualifications required by coast officers and gaugers were literacy and numeracy. Form-filling, letter-writing and calculations (especially in the case of excise staff) were essential components of the job. Whether there was any pre-employment educational test is not known. Boatmen substituting for tide-waiters had to be able to read and write. The surviving church records suggest that all or almost all boatmen could at least read. Not all boatmen could write, however, as the following extract from the minutes for 1765 shows:

> The board, having received a certificate in the name of David McNeal, coxon of the Baldoyle barge, on their order of trial of Thomas Sutherd for the employment of boatmen.
>
> Write to the surveyor of that barge to let the board know why the certificate was not made by him, and as the board understand that McNeal cannot write, to report who signed his name to the certificate.[6]

A further attempt to assess the educational levels of Fingal officers was made by comparing the names in a database designed for this study with those in *Alumni Dublinenses*, the list of alumni of Trinity College, Dublin.[7] This indicated that an estimated 5–10 per cent of officers of all grades who served in Fingal had attended the college before entering the service with the lower figure appearing to be the more probable. Several of these officers seem to have left the college without taking degrees. It is reasonable to assume, therefore, that officers had a good elementary education (probably what we would today call a second-level education) but that few of them had pursued their studies further.

Boatmen were required to be competent seamen. In January 1763 the minutes noted a letter from Captain Mercer, inspector of the revenue boats:

> proposing that whatever person is recommended for a boatman's employment should not only stand an examination, but be carried to sea at least a week's cruise and a certificate on oath returned by the surveyor that he is a thorough seaman and well qualified to be a boatman, and never if possible to exceed forty years of age, which trial ought not to be made in the port they are recommended from but in Dublin.[8]

This shows that some form of local examination of a boatman's capabilities was in force prior to 1763. Following Mercer's recommendation the commissioners had the following advertisement inserted in the newspapers:

> Young able seamen, being wanted in several of the revenue's barges in this kingdom, the commissioners of his majesty's revenue give notice, that they will give commissions to such seamen as can be well recommended and produce certificates of their sobriety and honesty. The salary of a king's boatman is twenty pounds a year. – N.B. It will be required that they undergo a trial in a week's cruise on board some of the barges belonging to the Port of Dublin, and obtain a certificate from the surveyor of that barge that they are able seamen and capable of working a wherry. By order of the commissioners.[9]

This is, perhaps, the only clear indication of a shortage of recruits to the service that emerged during the period. It also shows that sobriety was a valued quality in an aspiring boatman.

Recruits to the service seem to have come from a wide variety of backgrounds ranging from the younger sons of gentry families to the sons and brothers of serving officers. The normal procedure for a young man seeking employment in the service was to apply to be instructed in a specified branch of the revenue service. Once admitted to be instructed, the new customs officer could expect to spend about two to two and a half months learning the job. Training seems to have taken a number of forms including, for example, the working through of exercises on form-filling, the calculation of duties and the study of the legislation and policy as enunciated in 'general letters'. There are some surviving manuscripts which provide an insight into what the officers were expected to do.[10] These are in the form of detailed job descriptions. They date from the period *c.*1687–1702.

No evidence of a competency test on completion of training has been found for customs officers but in the case of a gauger a certificate of competence in the art of gauging was required from the officer's surveyor confirming that a gauger had 'surveyed constantly for one month with the most able expert officer in his survey'.[11] As a further precaution a gauger was appointed initially in a supernumerary capacity at a lower salary than that of a full gauger. If satisfactory he was later promoted to full gauger, normally by seniority within province. Considerable care was taken with the training of officers, particularly excise officers who had to work alone, often in a hostile environment.

Following completion of his training an officer expected to be appointed to a permanent post. Appointments were made by the resident commissioners in turn. Boatmen were also formally appointed by the commissioners in turn but the appointments were generally made on the recommendations of local surveyors who knew the applicants. Sometimes these appointments were 'for services rendered' but it is clear that many of the appointees had already served in a temporary or supernumerary capacity and their abilities were known.

As soon as possible after his appointment to his station, or after his appointment to a new station in the case of a transfer or promotion, generally within a matter of days, the officer formally took the oath of trust, an oath to perform the duties of his office diligently, faithfully and impartially, and was granted a commission which empowered him to carry out his duties. He then proceeded to his station. An officer arriving in a new station, who was already a serving officer, was normally granted from one to three weeks' leave to remove his family or settle his affairs. Even allowing for the difficulties of travel this leave allowance appears to have been quite generous. However, obtaining accommodation in a new station was often difficult. From the operational point of view it presented serious problems since most coast officers and gaugers appear to have used their homes as a working base. Purpose-built offices/stores, called 'watch-houses' were, however, provided in Clontarf, Malahide and Skerries. Many difficulties arose with the watch-houses over the

9. Dublin Bay, c.1747, showing Clontarf and Howth in the background
(Courtesy National Library of Ireland)

years and, as usual, even the most minor requests for repairs or supplies had to be submitted to the commissioners. Thanks to these submissions we know something about the individual watch-houses.

The commissioners obviously expected a certain minimum standard of maintenance since in 1717 they appointed Henry Berry, who had been dismissed, and later his widow, to keep the Clontarf watch-house clean and look after it.[12] Candles were usually supplied by the housekeeper from the commissioners' own store ('six dozen pounds' for Clontarf in 1717) while the local officers were usually allowed to purchase coal locally provided the purchase had been sanctioned.[13] The reason for this concession seems to have been the officers' local knowledge. They knew when coal had been landed and when it was available at a cheap rate. They tended to purchase in summer or early autumn. In 1722 the commissioners decided to close the Clontarf watch-house and began the process of assigning the Clontarf officers to named posts within the station's geographic area.[14]

The location of the Skerries watch-house, for which there is a record of the purchase of coal as early as 1719, seems to have led to few disciplinary or other problems.[15] The reason for this may have been that it was situated in a relatively isolated area on Haven Island, now known as Red Island, and that the surveyor lived close by. Coals, candles and other items were supplied to it from time to time. Repairs were carried out in 1742 and some further minor repairs in 1753.[16] Serious damage was caused by what was described as a 'violent hurricane' in October 1763.[17] The surveyor, Frederick Conyngham, reported that the king's house there had suffered greatly by the storm and that there was not a place in it that was not 'overflowed with rain', and that there was not a slater in the place to repair it. When the final bills for repairs to the buildings in the complex reached the commissioners nearly two years later they were horrified at the vast increase in the cost, £406 9*s*. 0½*d*., over the original estimate of £62 18*s*. 5*d*.[18] In fact, payment of the surveyor's salary was stopped pending enquiries. This order was rescinded on receipt of a report by Mr. Smyth, surveyor of the revenue buildings, that 'everything done was necessary nor is it yet complete without having the kitchen chimney rebuilt which will cost about eight guineas'.

The Skerries watch-house is marked on Rocque's map of 1760 .[19] It is more clearly shown on Scalé and Richards' map of 1765 (Figure 8).[20] There is a complex of three buildings, one of which was probably the surveyor's house. The watch-house was situated close to the harbour and commanded views to the north, east and south. Apart from its exposure to the frequent storms, its location must have been almost perfect from an operational point of view.

The situation regarding the watch-house in Malahide was rather different. It was first mentioned in 1725 when the newly-established and energetic riding surveyor, John Briscoe, suggested that a barge be stationed there and a watch-house rented at 40*s*. a year.[21] When, however, he requested permission to pay the rent due on the watch-house in February 1732 the commissioners wrote to him to know 'what occasion there is for the said watch-house, and what orders have been given from time to time about it and whether observed'.[22] His answer must have satisfied the commissioners because they decided to keep the watch-house for one year longer.[23] Two years later, when the rent again became due, they decided to continue to pay it.[24] In the meantime a decision had been taken to transfer the Bray barge to Malahide to combat smuggling and the question of arming the boats had also arisen.[25] A watch-house at Malahide had become essential. In November 1735 the watch-house was reported to be in a ruinous condition and the commissioners decided that another house should be rented.[26] This coincided with a period of serious indiscipline at the station. It was almost ten years before the question of building a new watch-house at Malahide arose again.[27] A detailed submission by the surveyor, Balthazar Cramer, gives a vivid account of what the working (and living) conditions of the officers were like. He claimed

> that the king's watch-house there [Malahide], in which the surveyor must dwell, (there not being any other place to accommodate him) is so old and rotten as not worth repairing; the walls are mud and tumbling down; that the present situation of the watch house is very inconvenient, having neither a view of the barge nor sea, and next door to an alehouse where all the persons who are spies upon the officers resort, and they can't stir

> without their knowledge, which may prove very detrimental to the revenue; and prays the board's order to build a new watch-house at the back of a place called the Ball Yard and will be only an additional rent of twenty shillings a year. He encloses two estimates, one by James Johnston, amounting to £215 10*s.* 8½*d.* and the other by John Hyndman.[28]

Johnston's estimate was accepted and the building of the new watch-house went ahead. Later, arrangements were made to add a coal-yard and a necessary-house (privy).[29] Work was slow and by December 1746 the plastering of the watch-house was still unfinished.[30] It is hardly surprising that drunkenness and indiscipline among the boatmen continued during this period.[31] In March 1747 a further problem arose when Cramer sought permission to add a further building to bark (dye and preserve) his sails.[32] This time the commissioners refused saying that they expected 'that the barking-pan be fixed up in some part of the present building'. The pan was provided but even this exceeded the estimate.[33] The surveyor, Thomas Wray, was directed to provide inside shutters for the windows in 1748.[34] In 1751 another surveyor, John Adamson, was still having problems. He reported that, 'in the late hurricane', not only had he lost the six-oared boat, but that the king's house and watch-house were 'stripped, the roofs fallen in and the windows broken'.[35] When he submitted several tradesmen's estimates for repairs to the house and watch-house the commissioners at first balked at but, having considered the cost of slating, finally agreed to his spending £18 11*s.* 9*d.* on thatching the watch-house.[36] Further disasters were to follow. Adamson reported in 1755

> That the walls of the out-offices in which the spare rigging and stores of the king's barge were kept, are fallen, together with the bog house, &c. and several breaches made in the roofs of the houses and watch-house; that the windows want glazing, painting and puttying; also that some new doors, locks and keys are wanting.[37]

Adamson also reported that 'Henry Cotter, who now holds the land on which the watch-house stands, demands twenty guineas fine for a renewal of the lease and a rent of twelve pounds a year for the future'. A schedule of deeds in the Public Records Office at Kew lists a deed dated 21 April 1746 which cites the lease of a watch-house at Malahide for twenty-one years from 26 December 1745 at a rent of £5 per annum from Henry Cotter to Balthazar Cramer.[38] This seems to have been Henry Cotter, boatman, who served continuously from 1738 until his resignation in 1759 despite being threatened with dismissal for insolence in 1746.[39] Naturally the commissioners could not accede to a rent demand of £12 per annum (instead of £5). They allowed some limited repairs and ordered Adamson to lay up the stores of the barge in some part of the house. Eventually they were persuaded to pay for the full repairs when it was pointed out that it would have been impossible to live there in winter if the work had not been done.[40] Problems with the watch-house continued however. Further repairs and thatching were carried out in 1762 and 1763.[41] In March 1763 an opportunity to locate the Malahide watch-house, the surveyor's house and houses for the crew in one place presented itself when the commissioners decided to lease four acres of meadow and four new houses for the crew from Edmond Curtis.[42] In July 1764, with the Cotter lease nearing its expiry, enquiries were initiated to find out if a new watch-house was required.[43] Repairs and extensions to a house on a new site owned by Edmond Curtis were sanctioned in the following December, thus providing the opportunity to break the association with Cotter.[44] The building work was completed by the end of 1765.[45] In summary, the development of a convenient but self-contained, if somewhat isolated, revenue complex in Skerries seems to have happened early and to have been rather fortuitous. The planned Malahide complex was developed only after revenue morale had suffered greatly through the intermingling of officers and smugglers in the earlier houses and other premises in the town.

Moving from consideration of the physical working conditions on land to the actual duties of the posts we are in a certain amount of difficulty. Unlike the large stations such as those at Ringsend, near Dublin, and Cork, none of the Fingal customs stations provided the full range of grades. The legislation was broad enough to allow a fair degree of flexibility not just between stations but also between grades. As early as 1701 we find that Thomas Jones, waiter, was asked to certify the days that boatmen remained on board vessels putting in at Skerries, so that they might have an additional 12*d.* a day for their 'extraordinary services'.[46] Jones, himself, was clearly fulfilling the duties previously (and subsequently) carried out by a surveyor while his boatmen were, on occasion, acting as tide-waiters. In the smaller stations the functions carried out by the waiters (later coast officers) appear to have been an amalgam of the duties of riding officer and land-waiter.

The duties of riding officers are described as follows in a manuscript ('An essay towards the methodical collecting of their majesties' revenue in Ireland ...') which seems to have been compiled in the 1690s or early 1700s and which describes, in particular, procedures in the larger stations:

> The riding officers on the coast being only officers of prevention and they being the first that see any ships, their duty is first which is wheresoever their station or district is appointed them that they make the most convenient place thereof for viewing the coast to be the place of their abode or habitation. They are to keep a horse and to be constantly on the shore side either on foot or on horseback that so they may see any vessels or boats that come near the shore and if they see any boats come ashore they are immediately to repair to the place and examine them and if they find any goods they are to seize the same and send or bring them with all

> convenient speed to their majesties' store. If there be any vessels or ships sailing near the shore, they are to ride along the coast still keeping sight of her till they meet the officer who is in the next riding so that and when they have so done they are to give charge of her to him and enter the same in a pocket book (in which book they are to keep a journal of their ridings and what ship they see, where they meet their fellow officers and so return). They are also to be very careful in examining all fishing boats that belong to any place, or shall come ashore in their riding. When the riding officers on the coast have watched the ship so far that she arrives in any bay or road, they are to give notice [to] all the tide-surveyors office[s], who in all probability, if it be in the daytime, will have discovered her before the news can come to them by the coast.[47]

This very early description of the riding officers' duties seems to correspond very closely with the functions carried out by the coast officers (originally called 'waiters'). Two aspects of their conditions of service are emphasised; the requirement that they live close to their stations and the requirement to keep a horse.

Occasionally the commissioners issued very precise instructions about residence as when in 1698 Mr. Stephens of Clontarf was ordered 'to make his abode at the ferry-boat over against the Lord Mayor's [presumably an inn], Mr. ffarthing at the Sheds of Clontarf'.[48] When the coast officer at Rush, Philip Wenman, was on leave in England in 1702 his colleague, Richard Davis of Portrane, was ordered to take charge of Rush as well as Portrane and 'to make Rush his residence'.[49] Sometimes the commissioners took exceptional measures to ensure that their directions were complied with. For example, they granted Henry Berry an advance of £20 to build a house at Clontarf, stipulating that 50*s*. a quarter was to be stopped out of his salary until the debt was repaid.[50] Very occasionally the commissioners relaxed their strict rules. In 1724 William Roberts, coast officer at Portrane, was permitted to live in Donabate as he was unable to find any house or accommodation at Portrane.[51] The commissioners were satisfied 'that Donabate lies convenient to his business and that from thence he may have a full view of the coast'.

Great emphasis was placed on the duty of keeping a horse. In 1696 the commissioners granted leave to Charles ffrowde, coast officer at Newhaven 'to come to Dublin to look after and prosecute a fellow that stole his horse'.[52] Thomas Jones, who was waiter at Skerries in 1701 during the period when the station did not have a surveyor, successfully sought an increase in salary as he was 'at extraordinary charges in living on the island [Skerries or Haven Island, now the Red Island peninsula, linked at that time by the Dorn or causeway to the mainland] and having no convenience of a stable for his horse, which he must provide'.[53] There were occasional riding accidents as, for example, when Henry Berry of Clontarf was injured in 1712.[54] In 1749 Thomas Wahab of Newhaven successfully petitioned that his surgeon's and his own expenses be paid since he 'had the misfortune, by his horse falling down a precipice to break his collar bone and dislocate his shoulder'.[55] The coast officers do not appear to have been granted any special allowance for keeping their horses. On the other hand, when James Tanner, a tide-waiter, supplied the place of Josiah Spranger at Portrane in 1713, he was allowed a horse during Spranger's absence.[56] At times the commissioners had a great deal of difficulty in enforcing the regulations about keeping horses. William Johns (Newhaven) was suspended in 1738 for a number of misdemeanors, including the fact that 'he keeps no horse'.[57] In 1747 the commissioners expressly ordered three officers, Daniel Ivie (Rush), and Oliver Zouch and Digby Walker (Clontarf) to do so.[58] In April 1749 two of them, Ivie and Walker had still failed to comply with the direction and were superannuated.[59] Even the unestablished preventive officers were heavily dependent on their horses. Samuel Gladwin was granted compensation (£10) for the houghing of a cow and a horse in 1757.[60] He claimed that he had 'not a horse to attend his duty, nor a cow to support his family'.

The other large group of customs employees in Fingal consisted of the boatmen and coxons. The 'Essay' already mentioned describes the boatmen's duties as follows:

> The duty of the watermen is to look after their boats, to keep them afloat in places where it may be done and in other places to lay them at the most convenient quays and docks where they may float soon and may lie securely. They are, when on shore, by turns to watch at the tide-surveyor's office, and they are also to be ready on all occasions both by night and day to attend the boats and obey such orders and directions as shall from time to time be given them by the surveyor.[61]

Strangely, the actual duties involved in sailing the boats are not mentioned. Perhaps these duties were just too obvious or perhaps they were much simpler in the early days when boatmen were needed to ferry surveyors and tide-waiters to the larger ships anchored some way from the shore or to the offshore islands rather than to chase smugglers at sea. The days of the large customs barges were still far in the future.

What was involved in looking after the boats? Who made and mended the sails? Who barked them? Who cleaned the boats? We have no precise details about the day-to-day work of boatmen, nor have we a record of the incidental expenses incurred by the respective stations, so that we must rely solely on what can be inferred from the minutes. Canvas (one of the items which was purchased centrally) was supplied by the yard from time to time but there is no mention of the sanctioning of labour costs to have the sails made. Similarly, items such as furze, mops, hog's lard and tallow were frequently purchased to clean the boats but there is no mention of who carried out the work. In the absence of more precise information we can only surmise that these tasks were carried out by the boatmen. The first reference found to the barking of the sails of a revenue boat in Fingal is a direction to George Boyd, surveyor, in 1735 to have the Malahide barge graved and the sails barked and to certify the cost.[62] This almost certainly means that the job was done locally by the boatmen or by skilled tradesmen. By 1761 the barking of sails was certainly regarded as the boatmen's duty as the following extract from the minutes shows:

> Richard Lewis, deputy surveyor of the Greencastle barge, his petition that he got the barge's sails barked at Skerries according to the board's order and praying to be paid the expense amounting to £3 10*s*. 3½*d*.; and Captain Mercer [inspector of the revenue boats] having reported that all the articles are charged reasonably except half a guinea to the crew whose business it is to do the work.[63]

Certain other tasks, for example, repairs, graving and carpentry work such as the replacement of masts, were certainly carried out at the main revenue depot at Ringsend or by local tradesmen. In 1720 the surveyor-general reported that 'it will save a considerable yearly expense in the repairs of the king's barge and tackling to appoint a coxon to take care thereof and to be answerable for the same if any damage should happen by his neglect'.[64] The appointment of coxons placed the responsibility for the care of the boats clearly on the local crews.

As has already been stated boatmen sometimes performed the duties of tide-waiter. At a later stage tide-waiters were supplied, as needed, in a temporary capacity, to Skerries and Malahide from the major port at Ringsend.[65] A detailed description of the tide-waiter's duties is given in the 'Essay'.[66] They were expected to go and stay on board ships while they were in port, to search passengers and seamen boarding and leaving the ships, to check all goods being brought on board or ashore and to search and rummage ships. Tide-waiters were needed in harbours where there was a large amount of normal trade. Their presence freed the surveyor and the boatmen to wage a more active war against smuggling at sea. The list of duties also gives some idea of the range of duties which must have been undertaken by the boatmen before the appointment of tide-waiters.

When John Briscoe was appointed in 1722 in a temporary capacity for one year as the first riding surveyor in Fingal he had supervisory duties extending far beyond those of a riding officer.[67] Referring to the County Dublin coast the commissioners felt

> either that that part of the coast is not sufficiently guarded or that the coast officers stationed there do not perform their duty as they ought. In order, therefore, to keep the said officers strictly to their duty and to guard more effectually that coast, ordered that Mr. John Briscoe be appointed surveyor to inspect the coast from Dublin to Gormanstown for one year.

Two years later Briscoe's new post was established as a permanent one.[68]

Turning to the excise the gauger's duty is described succinctly in a 1693 manuscript, the author of which is believed to have been Lord Chief Baron Hely.[69]

> The gauger goes round his walks twice every week, and takes an account of every brewing within it, and of the quantity of each sort of liquors made [in] it, each brewing in that compass this he reduces into gallons according to which the duty was charged.
>
> The surveyor goes after the gauger once a month, and takes private notes in his pocket book of the several brewings in that month, and the quantities and qualities brewed which are compared with the gauger's book, and every month both sign a return to the collector, who reduces the gallons into money and receives it from the people.

There is a more detailed account of the gauger's duty in relation to inland excise in another fragmentary manuscript compiled around 1694 which reads:

> For the securing and collecting of this duty gaugers are appointed in convenient walks to take the true dimensions of such vessels as the common brewer or retailer makes use of to compute and to take an account of the respective quantity brewed, distilled and sold by them, of which two vouchers are made, abstracted from the gauger's original entries in his pocketbook and examined by the surveyor: specifying the time and number of gallons of either sort brewed by each person, one of which is monthly sent to the commissioners and delivered to the examinator and the other is delivered as a charge (due from the several brewers and retailers) on the collectors, who do appoint monthly offices at certain days in divers places within their districts, to collect and levy the same.[70]

The gaugers evidently had to have a reasonably good grasp of basic mathematics and an ability to get on with people. They generally worked alone and were vulnerable to various temptations as well as to hostile groups. However, a system of checks and balances had been instituted to identify discrepancies in reports. In October 1721 the surveyor for County Dublin, William Hodson, was dismissed for a number of offences, including some committed in Fingal. The principal surveyor reported that

> he has returned false accounts of surveying and taking stocks and gauges in several places and houses which do not appear in the officers' books, as particularly July 17 that the surveyor stocked Corduff, Rush and Donabate, August the 1st that he stocked Corduff walk round, August 3 and 4 that he stocked the said walk round ... July 13 in Finglas walk that he stocked one retailing brewer and met the officer, the same day that he stocked at Finglas a common brewer ... July 25 that in Swords walk

> he stocked the town of Swords in the officer's book, whom he met there and no such stock was taken. That there has been no stock made that quarter by the surveyor at the town of Malahide, where are two retailing brewers and one non-brewing retailer . . .[71]

A report on another instance of neglect of duty, which led to the dismissal of John Ford (Finglas) in March 1729, tells us more about the checks that were used to keep the gaugers in order as well as a little about the area at that time.[72] Thomas Skellern reported

> that on the 2 instant he [Thomas Skellern] went to a patron at Stradbally in Finglas walk, and enquired whether John Ford, the gauger, had been there, either that day or the day before, and found he had not. He surveyed a widow who had been a non-brewing retailer of that place, and found she had brewed, and had with her 117 gallons of ale of her own brewing, part of it concealed; she said the officer had not been with her for a considerable time. He went to Greenoge, where are two non-brewing retailers, and found by the visit paper that the officer had not surveyed the place since the 3 of February; that upon surveying Kilsallaghan, St. Margaret's and that round to Finglas he found the officer had not been there since the 3 of February. That at Finglas, his place of residence, he made strict enquiry for him, and could not find he had been there since Saturday the first, this being the third; at this time it was morn 11, and his brewer at work, the surveyor waited for the officer but did not see him till nine at night, when he secured his book and found two surveys entered, one the 10 and the other the 20 of last month, on those places which Mr. Skellern had surveyed, though the visit papers (as aforesaid) showed none such there, which makes it appear that the visits were forged.

Both customs and excise officers were expected to make seizures. Time and time again the commissioners reprimanded the officers for their failure to make a sufficient number of seizures and the making of seizures was regarded by contemporaries as one of the principal indicators of success. Since the seizure books have not survived we are dependent on contemporary newspapers to enable us to get some idea of the level of seizures. A detailed analysis has been made of seizures by the crews of the large customs stations which had barges, Skerries, Malahide and Baldoyle (originally Portrane) for the six years 1759–64. The analysis shows that in all three stations tea, brandy and tobacco were the main commodities seized. There is insufficient information to calculate the quantities and/or value of the goods but, as there is no reason to believe that the newspapers reported selectively, it is possible to estimate the numbers of seizures made. Table 4 summarises the position for the three stations.

While some of the seizures were undoubtedly valuable, the king's moiety, as well as payments to informers and other expenses, had to be deducted

Table 4. Numbers of reported seizures by customs crews 1759–1764 (incl.)

Year	*Number of seizures reported in selected newspapers*		
	Skerries crew	*Malahide crew*	*Baldoyle crew*
1759	23	4	
1760	10	6	
1761	14	5	5
1762	15	4	5
1763	10	5	5
1764	8	2	2

Sources: *The Dublin Gazette, The Public Gazetteer, The Freeman's Journal*

before the proceeds were divided among eight to twelve people. The extra money earned was no doubt a welcome addition to salary but it was unlikely that anyone made a fortune, even in an exceptionally good year.

The routine duties laid down in the legislation were not the only activities of officers. Life in the Fingal service had its darker side which affected both the customs and the excise officers. This is evidenced by the violence which has had such an influence on the folklore of the area, especially in north Fingal, where stories of conflicts between the revenue men and the smugglers survive to the present day. These stories have been told in a number of places as, for example, in the Schools Manuscript Collection 1937–8, which was compiled by the children of the 1930s, with the help of their teachers, from the recollections of older people in their neighbourhoods.[73] A more recent collection of stories by adults about smuggling in Fingal has been published as an audio-cassette.[74] But can the documents tell us anything more?

Table 5. Reported incidents by decade and type of occurrence, 1719–1765

	Type of incident					
Decade	*Killing*	*Wounding violence and assault*	*Threats, abuse and obstruction*	*Attacks on animals*	*Attacks on boats and other property*	*Total*
1710–1719			1			1
1720–1729		1	1		1	3
1730–1739	4	8				12
1740–1749	2	13	1			16
1750–1759	3	7		2	2	14
1760–1765 (6 years)	1	11	5	1		18
TOTAL	10	40	8	3	3	64

Sources: P.R.O., CUST 1, and contemporary newspapers

An attempt has been made to analyse contemporary material available in the minutes and in certain newspapers. Table 5 shows the number of reported cases by decade of occurrence (the earliest incident occurred in 1719) and by type of incident while Table 6 shows the same data analysed by place of occurrence and alleged perpetrator.

Table 5 shows that at least 78 per cent of the cases involved death or very serious physical injury. Since the revenue minutes are complete for the period 1717 to August 1753 and almost complete for the period from September 1754 to the end of 1765, the sharp increase in violent incidents from the 1720s to the 1730s cannot be explained by gaps in information. While the figures show that one to two violent incidents occurred each year on average, it seems likely that they do not reflect the full extent of the violence which flared up from time to time. The fact that some incidents appear in newspapers but not in the minutes suggests that either they were discussed by the commissioners but not minuted or that they were dealt with informally or at a lower level, for example, by the collector for County Dublin. In a small number of cases the omission can be accounted for through the non-survival of the particular minute-books.

Table 6 shows that one-third of the incidents involved either internal disputes or attacks by revenue officers on others. It also shows that no one area had a monopoly of violence.

Table 6. Reported incidents by place of occurrence and alleged perpetrator, 1719–1765

	Allegedly perpetrated by			
Place of occurrence	*An officer on a fellow-officer*	*Revenue officers and/or associates on others*	*Others on officers and/or associates*	*Total*
At sea			2	2
Baldoyle			4	4
Clontarf/Ballybough/ Raheny		1	2	3
Donabate/ Portrane		1	3	4
Finglas			1	1
Garristown	1		6	7
Howth/Ireland's Eye		1	3	4
Malahide/Feltrim	2	1	3	6
Rush/Loughshinny		2	5	7
Skerries	1	1	4	6
Swords/Cloghran/ Ballymadrough		2	4	6
Not specified		3	11	14
TOTAL	4	12	48	64

Sources: P.R.O., CUST 1, and contemporary newspapers

One of the most vivid and interesting accounts of the difficulties under which the officers and their families had to live is found neither in the minutes nor in the contemporary newspapers but in a single surviving volume of reports by the revenue solicitor.[75] This account, which illustrates the pressures, not just on the officers but also on their families, reads:

> In obedience date the 16th November inst. on the petition of Laurence Kean . . . On the 10th day of June last past Mary Hudson, wife of Alexander Hudson, coast officer of Portrane in the County of Dublin, gave in examinations before Sir Robert Echlin, Baronet, in which she swears that three persons, whose names she knew not, on said day broke and forcibly entered into the room of Alexander Hudson in the house of Richard Sankey of Rush in the County of Dublin aforesaid, forcibly carried away four casks of leaf tobacco and one anchor of brandy, seized by said Hudson, and that a person then in custody, who confessed his name to be Laurence Kean, was the person who carried away the first cask of said tobacco and the rest of the said persons carried away the remainder and at the same time beat and abused the said Mary Hudson in a most violent manner upon which examinations an indictment was found against the said Laurence Kean and several others unknown for a riot and rescue of the said tobacco and said Laurence Kean is to be tried on said indictment this present Michaelmas term, being found that since the indictment was found against the said Kean he turned King's evidence and gave examinations against Andrew Colgan, James Murphy and Peter Drew as parties concerned with him in said rescue, upon which a bill was found against them and the said Peter Drew, being taken on a capias issued on the said indictment, his trial came on the last Commission of Oyer and Terminer for the County of Dublin, upon which indictment it was necessary to prove the officer and commissions who seized the goods in order to inflict the punishment prescribed by the statute. One of the commissioners' names, which was formerly signed to the said commissions, being so obliterated that it could not be proved to a commission signed by three commissioners, the jury acquitted him but immediately at the said commissioner's second indictment was sent up against the said Peter Drew and other for a riot and assault on the said Mary Hudson and on the evidence of said Mary Hudson and said Laurence Kean proving the said Drew to be one of the persons concerned in the said riot and assault, he was accordingly found guilty and sentenced to six months' imprisonment and five pound fine.

This incident, which does not appear in the minutes of the commissioners, must have taken place between 1742 and 1744 when Alexander Hudson was stationed at Portrane. In 1745 Alexander himself was assaulted 'in the execution of his duty'.[76] The family's stay in Fingal ended sadly. The minutes of 2 November 1745 contain the following:

> Complaint having been made to the board that Alexander Hudson, coast officer at Portrane, had differed with the other officers, and there is reason to apprehend the revenue may suffer by such dissensions, ordered therefore that the said Hudson, and George Glover, coast officer at Arklow, exchange stations for the service of the revenue.[77]

The violence which flared up from time to time resulted in applications by the revenue commissioners to the lords justices for army assistance. Applications to station troops at Garristown to assist the gauger there were made on a number of occasions. The exact circumstances under which troops were first quartered in the coastal area are not known. The army may have been deployed there during the summer of 1760, a period for which the revenue commissioners' minutes are missing. In November 1760 the following entry appears in the minutes.

> The secretary to write to Cornet Burton, commanding the Light Horse quartered at Swords, Lieutenant Burton, commanding at Rush and Cornet Gore, commanding at Skerries, that the board have been informed that the revenue officers are not so active as they should be in making seizures and pursuing the smugglers with the assistance of the Light Horse which the government have been pleased to quarter there for that purpose, wherefore, when run goods are carried in parties through that country to the knowledge of any of the Light Horse, and that no attempts are made by the revenue officers to seize them, the board request those gentlemen will send to them any of the soldiers who can give evidence thereof upon oath.[78]

It is not known if any of the army officers mentioned informed on the revenue officers. However, someone did, as the following extract from the September 1761 minutes, which contains a hint of desperation, shows:

> Write severally to Walter Davis, coast surveyor, and Mathew Dowling, surveyor of excise on the coast from Dublin to Drogheda, that the board have received good information that smuggling from the Isle of Man is carried on upon that coast with more, rather than less, violence since the Light Horse were quartered there, that the board impute this solely to the neglect or corruption of the officers and their declining to make use of that force which the government have appointed there for the support of the revenue; wherefore the board direct them to go round to every officer of the coast and excise, and to acquaint them that as the long nights are now approaching and the smugglers will have more oppor-

> tunities of running from the Isle of Man if the officers do not exert themselves so as to destroy the smuggling trade before Christmas next, they may be prepared to quit that station, as the board are determined at least to remove them to some other part of the kingdom; and the surveyors are to give each officer on the coast a copy of this order.[79]

Walter Davis, the riding surveyor, informed the commissioners that the 'Light Horse are so quartered as to be of little use to some of the coast officers'.[80] On his recommendation the ten soldiers in the northern part of the area (and east Meath) were redeployed in small groups.[81] In 1763 Sir Edward Newenham, collector for County Dublin, requested that a sergeant, corporal and twelve soldiers be stationed at Rush since nobody in the area had 'come to pay their licence for last year'.[82] When, in the following year, the commissioners suggested that these troops might be withdrawn as four regiments were being sent to the West Indies, Newenham successfully requested a doubling of the force 'as this is the time they will be much wanted, the boats from the Isle of Man being expected in very soon, and that, from the spirit he now finds in the mob, he is certain the officers dare not do their duty'.[83] The army itself was not immune from attack. Corporal George Scott and four other soldiers sought compensation on the grounds that 'in July 1764 being ordered to convey William Higley [a well-known smuggler] to Newgate they were attacked by a furious mob and in the affray Scott the Corporal's skull was fractured, under which he languished a considerable time in a miserable way and still continues so, that the rest of the party were cut and wounded in a desperate manner . . .'.[84] The army was little more successful than the revenue officers.

The working lives of the customs and excise officers were a mixture of routine tasks and highly dangerous encounters with law-breakers as well as with the elements. It is remarkable that, despite the frequent reports of the drowning of officers in other areas, no record has been found of the death by drowning of a Fingal officer in the period covered by this study. The encounters with smugglers on land and sea demanded a loyalty, camaraderie and level of co-operation which, within and between some stations at least, was evident. The dangerous lives which the officers lived also required strong external support systems. These support systems will be examined in the next part.

Family, friends and the wider community

A tablet in Holmpatrick Church in Skerries reminds us that revenue officers had interests and responsibilities beyond those of the service. It reads as follows:

In memory
of ELIZABETH the Wife
of GEORGE WESTON Esqr
Surveyor of this Port, who departed
this life 18th July 1751,
And also
of Jane the Daughter of the said
GEORGE & ELIZABETH WESTON
Aged six months.

In this part I propose to examine, insofar as it is possible, the personal lives of the revenue officers and their families and their relationships with their churches and the wider community.

George Weston, who served in Fingal for more than thirty-three years, twenty-seven of which were spent in Skerries, was an Englishman from Berkeley in Gloucestershire. He made occasional, if infrequent, long visits to England throughout his career and on his resignation in 1761, returned to Berkeley where he died and was buried on 29 July 1774.[1] Details of his marriage have not been found – Elizabeth Weston may have been English – but it would seem that, after her death, he formed some kind of attachment to another Skerries woman, Ann Braithwaite, who later married Thomas Young of the city of Bath. In his will Weston made a generous bequest to provide for the education and bringing up of Ann's daughter, Elizabeth Charlotte Braithwaite. While by no means a regular participant in parish affairs – he attended two Church of Ireland vestry meetings in 1737 and 1760 – he was, nevertheless appointed supervisor of the roads in 1737, 1738, 1739, 1742 and 1760.[2] Weston was very much in the public eye. Details of the dramatic seizures made by him and his crew were reported regularly in the newspapers. Yet we know almost nothing about his private life.

Weston left practically the only tangible memorial to the service, apart from documents, which remains to us. It is perhaps significant that this memorial is to be found in the parish church. Before examining the personal

10. The Weston tablet, Holmpatrick Church, Skerries
(*Courtesy Mr Jack Benton, Balbriggan*)

and family lives of the customs and excise officers it may be useful to look at their association with that other powerful country-wide organisation, the established church, of which they were expected to be, at least nominally, members. This relationship was closer than the official records might lead one to believe.

While there were early dismissals in other areas it was some time before the Fingal officers felt the effects of the laws against the employment of Catholics.[3] Daniel Byrne, a Catholic boatman at Malahide was dismissed in 1741.[4] In January 1762 a number of Malahide boatmen were dismissed.[5] The reasons given for three of these dismissals, based on the report of Captain Mercer, inspector of the revenue boats, are of interest.

> William Evans is a good boatmen, but to his [Mercer's] knowledge and by the account of the surveyor and deputy is most riotous, drunken and disobedient and, when the surveyor reprimands him, he says he can get better bread by smuggling and there is good reason to think he is concerned and that he is married to a Papist and breeds his children Papists . . .
>
> Charles Betts . . . is a mutinous disorderly insolent refractory man and as he [Mercer] believes concerned with the smugglers . . . his wife is connected with the Rush smugglers, is a rigid Papist and breeds all her children in that profession . . .

> Peter Dugall is by all accounts a most notorious disobedient man and on all occasions refuses doing his duty and is a prejudice to the revenue by preventing harmony and good order among the crew . . . he and his sons keep cars and carry goods for the smugglers, which he could not deny when charged with, and that he is a Papist.

What Mercer omitted to state in his report, perhaps out of consideration for the sensibilities of the commissioners, was that Evans, Betts and Dugall had served for six, eleven and twenty-six years, respectively, in Malahide and that Betts and Dugall had served in other stations before their transfers to Malahide.

There were at least two other dismissals of former Fingal employees for reasons related in part to religion. William Orret, a former coast officer at Newhaven who had been promoted to the post of riding surveyor in Wexford, was dismissed in 1717 for cursing the bishop of Bangor and for drinking Dr. Sacherevell's health.[6] Henry Lovely, a Dun Laoghaire boatman, who had served for a short period in Skerries and who had been seriously wounded there in the course of a seizure, was dismissed in 1744 because he

> has a general bad character, and is believed would perjure himself on all occasions, has been detected of theft and strongly suspected to be in league with the smugglers and has often betrayed the officers when upon informations, is married to a Papist &c.[7]

An attempt has been made here to quantify, at least in a crude way, the relationship between the officers and their church by using the information contained in surviving vestry books. Vestry books for the parishes of Howth (Baldoyle, Howth and Sutton), Clontarf and Garristown do not survive for the period.

The method adopted was to extract the names of the officers who were stationed in particular parishes, for a period, no matter how short, after the date of commencement of the earliest surviving vestry books for those parishes and up to the end of 1765. Attendance at vestry meetings was noted as was any office held, such as that of churchwarden or supervisor/overseer of the roads. Many of the officers remained in their stations for just a short period of time. Since vestry meetings were not always held at regular intervals in the eighteenth century, since officers probably needed time to familiarise themselves with parish affairs and since some might have been prevented from attending by pressure of work or other reasons, those who were stationed in a particular place for three years or more were counted separately.

Table 7 shows that about 14 per cent of all officers showed some form of active interest in their church but if the twenty-seven participant officers are expressed as a proportion of 'long-stay' officers the percentage is much higher (33 per cent). There are reasons to believe that the table may understate participation slightly.

Table 7. Participation by customs and excise officers in parish affairs

Parish	*Stations covered*	*Total no. of officers in data set*	*No. who served for 3 years or more*	*At one or more meetings*	*Served as church-warden*	*Served as overseer or supervisor of roads*	*Total actively involved in parish affairs*
		Number of Officers					
Balrothery	Balrothery	1	1	1			1
Balrothery	Newhaven	6	2	2	1	1	2
Donabate	Portrane	14	8	1		1	1
Finglas	Finglas	27	7				
Holmpatrick	Skerries	41	32	15	4	5	15
Lusk	Corduff	8	1				
Lusk	Rush	9	4	1			1
Swords	Malahide	77	22	3		3	4
Swords	Swords	7	4	3	1		3
TOTAL		190	81	26	6	10	27

Source: Representative Church Body Library, Vestry books for the parishes of Balrothery, Donabate, Finglas, Holmpatrick, Lusk and Swords

Several vestrymen at this period indicated their presence by making their marks. The revenue officers, however, invariably signed the vestry books. This indicates that they could at least read and probably also had some writing ability.

The major factors which influenced participation seem to have been proximity to the church where the vestry was held and length of service. Participation was high in Swords and Skerries where church and station were located in the same town. Balrothery also had a high participation rate but the numbers are small and it is not known when the officer in Newhaven went to live in the growing town of Balbriggan, which would have been nearer to Balrothery Church. Those who lived in Malahide, Portrane, Rush and Corduff would have had to travel some distance to vestry meetings. In general, as one might expect, it is the longer-serving officers who attended vestries or undertook parish work. The more senior officers also tend to be over-represented. They probably had better transport, for example, horses, available. Skerries, where distance was not a problem, is, once again, an interesting exception. Several of the boatmen there took part in the work of the vestry and three of them, Thomas Tillotson Bolton, Thomas Griffin and John Willett, together with two former boatmen who had been promoted, Joshua and George Wahab, were churchwardens.

The church undoubtedly gave the lives of many officers a focal point. It also provided them with opportunities to meet the local gentry and other neighbours. Friendships were forged which often ended in marriage thus cementing the link with the local community and promoting its stability and development. Opportunities for upward mobility existed and were sometimes availed of. On the other hand, the service offered the church a great deal apart from loyal support. It provided a corps of literate people who were ready and willing to take on parish duties, which, at that time, extended far beyond attendance at church services. Participants in church affairs also linked their more lukewarm colleagues to the church.

Turning to the families of the officers we find that the revenue records offer us only an occasional and indirect glimpse of their private lives. To what extent did 'service families' exist? Clusters of unusual names suggest that they were common. A number of clusters occur in Fingal while unusual surnames occurring in Fingal can sometimes be found in other areas or in other branches of the service. The amount of direct evidence from the minutes is slight but there are some interesting references. Thomas Griesdale (Skerries and, later, Ringsend) and Samuel Griesdale were brothers.[8] The minutes tell us that Thomas Grumley was the son of John Grumley.[9] 'Grumley' is a common Fingal name although neither of these officers served in the area at this period. Lancelot Denton, transferred from Ringsend to Rush in 1725, was the son of a former tide-waiter at Ringsend, Thomas Denton.[10] When Thomas Disney, land-waiter, Newry, was appointed joint collector with his father in Galway in 1745, his brother George was appointed to replace him at Newry.[11] The brothers, Francis and John Disney, were appointed to Malahide in 1763 but it is not clear if they were also related to the Disneys of Galway and Newry.[12] John Adamson, surveyor, and his boatman son, also called John, served together in Malahide.[13] Richard Shaw, who served in several Fingal stations, had a son in the revenue service.[14] Occasionally relationships can be deduced from other sources. Nicholas Coddington, coast officer, Clontarf, was the nephew of Elizabeth, Lady Handcock, whose second husband was James Forth, secretary to the revenue commissioners.[15] It seems almost certain that John Gay, coast officer, Baldoyle, who was placed on the charity establishment at £14 per annum in March 1723, was the same John Gay who cut off his son, William, with a shilling in 1725. It also seems probable that his son was the William Gay who had been coast officer in Clontarf and Howth.[16] Perhaps the most telling indicator of the frequency of service relationships is to be found in the rules made in 1755 for the award of pensions which state:

> That no dismissed officer shall be ordered on the charity establishment, unless at the time of his dismissal, and that no person shall have the benefit of this fund if his son be appointed to succeed him in his employment.[17]

What kind of background did the officers have? Peter (or Pierre) Fraigneau, who was coast officer at Portrane from 1719 to 1724 was a French Protestant.[18] George Weston of Skerries was certainly English. In the absence of information to the contrary and as most of the English surnames can be found in Ireland at an earlier period, it seems reasonable to assume that the vast majority of the officers were Irish.

Socially, most of the officers belonged to lower middle-class families. Nicholas Coddington, who transferred from Clontarf to Drogheda in December 1720, was a member of a prominent Skerries gentry family and the founder of an even better-known Oldcastle, County Meath, family.[19] Sir Randall O'Neill, who served as coast officer in Rush from 1749, was a member of the family of the O'Neills of Clandeboye.[20] Apart from these two officers, there are few, if any, officers from well-known aristocratic or gentry families to be found in the Fingal lists.

An officer's period of service in Fingal could vary from a few weeks to over thirty years. Analysis of the length of time spent by each officer in a particular grade in a station shows that while the arithmetic mean of a period of service was 3½ years the median was only two years. As one might expect many officers were already married when they came to Fingal. The number of officers who obtained leave 'to remove their families' on transfer or exchange is evidence of this. Others, no doubt, married after they left the area. In the absence of church registers a perusal of Betham's Genealogical Abstracts yielded some information about the issue of marriage licences. Particularly interesting are the small number which show that boatmen were marrying into the local community. Table 8 shows two examples.

It is interesting that Joseph Jacob described himself or was described as a 'gentleman'. Thomas Griffin, another Skerries boatman, who married Ann Adams in Dublin City in 1760, was similarly described.[21] This designation occurs from time to time and may reflect the status which employment in the revenue service gave even its most junior officers.

While the marriage registers for Swords are not included in the Fingal Heritage Centre records for the period 1684–1765, the baptismal registers dating from 1705 (the only baptismal registers for the period for the Fingal area which survive) record the baptisms of several children who are almost certainly the children of Swords gaugers and Malahide customs staff.[22] Five children of the Malahide boatman, Henry Cotter, and his wife, Bridget, are listed as are three children of the Swords preventive officer, David Byas and his wife, Elizabeth.

Table 8. Some marriage licences issued to revenue officers

Groom	*Bride*	*Date licence issued*	*Betham Reference*
Jacob, Joseph, Skerries, Gent.	Murray, Mary, Parish of Holmpatrick	25 July 1749	5–26–144–355
Wheeler, John, Skerries, Mariner	Vaunce, Elizabeth, Parish of Holmpatrick	31 August 1748	5–26–88–242

Source: N.A., Betham's Genealogical Abstracts, Series V

Three children of the Malahide boatman and coxon, John Weldrick and his wife, Elizabeth, as well as four children of the Malahide boatman and coxon, John Davis, and his wife, Mary, also appear in the register. A number of other names appear which would require further research to confirm with certainty.

There is little information available on the education of officers' children. Probably not more than 5 per cent of the officers had attended Trinity College Dublin. This is hardly surprising as most of those who served in Fingal were in the junior grades of the service. What is rather more surprising is that only about 5 per cent of the officers had sons who attended Trinity. Probably few service families could have afforded to avail of higher education for their children. Access to higher education was not, apparently, a major factor in the upward mobility of families.

The main route to social advancement seems to have been through the revenue service itself or through other public services such as the army. Marriage and the gradual acquisition of land may also have been factors but the evidence found for this is slight.

One difficulty affecting family life which officers experienced was that of obtaining suitable accommodation. As early as 1699, John Daniel, gauger, Corduff, complained about being dispossessed of his lodging at Lusk.[23] William Roberts was unable to find a house at Portrane in 1724.[24] Two years later the same officer complained that he had received several insults and that there had been an attempted robbery at his house at Portrane.[25] In February 1738 Brothwell Lloyd, boatman, Skerries, petitioned for a transfer on the grounds that he had been 'threatened by the runners and grossly abused by them for exerting himself in the execution of his duty, that he dares not reside there [in Skerries] his life being in very great danger'.[26] An entry in the minutes for 1743 illustrates how dependent the revenue was on the goodwill of the local landlords.[27] It reads:

> Direct Mr. Boyd, surveyor of the Fingal coast, to wait on my Lord Howth to desire that he will permit Richard Shaw, coast officer, to reside in the town of Howth, which will be for the service of the revenue.

A problem of a different kind arose in 1744 when Langford Burleigh, surveyor, County Dublin, was reprimanded for 'not directing the gauger of Skerries [presumably the supernumerary gauger] to keep a register of the several places for brewing, working and storing drink brewed for sale and for suffering him to live in a public house'.[28] In 1745 the commissioners decided to rent a house for the use of the coast officers at Clontarf and to charge them half the rent.[29] On this occasion, however, the decision may have had more to do with the disciplinary difficulties they were experiencing with the individual officers than with any problem about finding lodgings. The surveyor's house at Malahide was also provided for him by the revenue.[30] In February 1763 Francis Drew, deputy surveyor at Malahide, informed the commissioners that

> there are no houses for the crew by which they are obliged to lodge in the smugglers' houses, who have a constant watch on them and when they are called together to go on duty the smugglers immediately send out boats, light fires and make other signals to warn the boats from the Isle of Man that the barge is gone to sea.[31]

A few weeks later Captain Mercer, inspector of the revenue boats, confirmed this account and proposed the leasing of four new houses and four acres of meadow from Edmond Curtis.[32] In sanctioning this the commissioners gave their opinion that

> the surveyor's duty at Malahide cannot be effectually done while there is such a connection between the smugglers and boatmen, and they know that a cruising barge cannot go out upon informations with that dispatch and secrecy which the service requires when the crew is to be collected from different parts of a town.

The larger customs stations such as Skerries, Malahide and Clontarf seem to have been reasonably well, if, in some instances, belatedly, catered for. The smaller centres were not so lucky. In July 1758 the minutes record:

> Randall O'Neill, coast officer at Rush, his petition setting forth the difficulties he labours under by the people at Rush refusing to give him a lodging, by which he has been forced to take a house at a double rent of eight pounds a year for payment of which Sir Henry Echlin's agent has now called upon him, and that he has been at great expense in repairing the said house, and praying relief.
>
> The board on consideration of the petitioner's particular situation and low circumstances, and that he is an active officer, direct that an order be made out to the collector to pay him eight pounds, and the petitioner is to pay his own rent.[33]

The commissioners also consented to pay for repairs to the gauger's house in Garristown in 1759.[34]

While the local people do not seem to have welcomed revenue officers and probably made life difficult for them, the number of reported attacks on property was relatively small by comparison with the number of attacks on the person. The smugglers seem to have been mainly interested in recovering seizures which they regarded as their property.

The attitude of the local gentry to the service was, to say the least, ambivalent. There are very occasional letters of thanks for assistance but the fact that special letters were sent to these men for doing what was, in effect, their duty suggests that this co-operation was relatively rare. Dixie Coddington (Skerries), who had been 'serviceable to the revenue on several occasions' received a letter of thanks in 1734 while Alexander Hamilton (Balbriggan) received one in 1741.[35] The local gentry and landowners were more frequently involved in making complaints. The minutes give the impression, however, that these gentlemen were more interested in asserting their status and authority than in seriously obstructing the officers in the execution of their duty, for example, one such complaint in 1717 resulted in the transfer from Portrane of John Maccabe

> who (upon the complaint of Ensign Adam Lynn of his having misbehaved himself by threatening and insulting the said Lynn and other gentlemen on Sunday night the 10 instant); that the earnest desire of the said Lynn [is] that the said Maccabe might not be dismissed, is appointed coast officer in the county of Wexford . . .[36]

In May 1753 Lord Howth complained that

> three persons calling themselves revenue officers armed with pistols and swords had compelled a car of his going to Howth to turn back and to carry a seizure they had made to Dublin.

One of the two Dublin city officers involved was suspended and the other, described as being very drunk, was dismissed but both the suspension and notice of dismissal were rescinded on Lord Howth's intervention.[37] But there were more serious incidents. William Bell, boatman at Skerries was dismissed

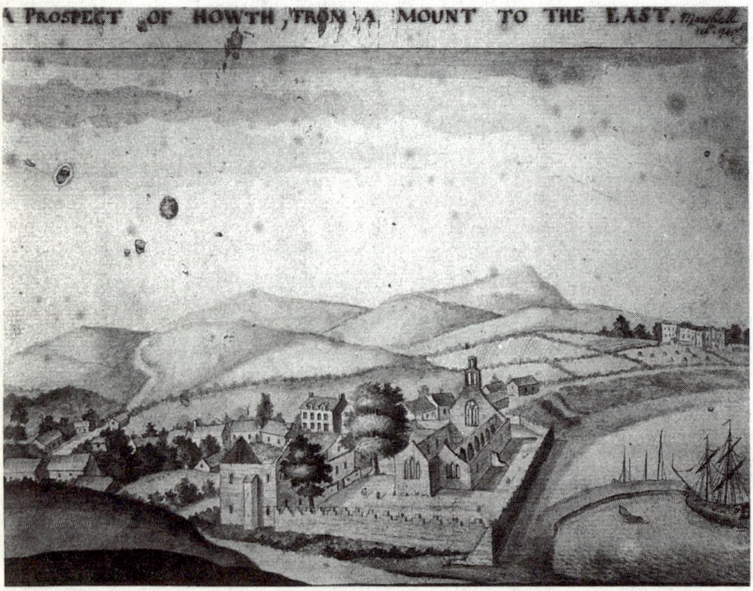

11. A prospect of Howth, one of the small harbours in the Port of Dublin, in 1745 (*Courtesy National Library of Ireland*)

in March 1726 for insulting the Hon. William St Lawrence while Charles Tomlinson, coast officer, Clontarf was transferred to Dundalk in March 1740 'having been very abusive to Captain Vernon and other gentlemen of the neighbourhood'.[38] There were some more sinister occurrences which showed just how influential the local gentry were. Lewis Howell, surveyor, Skerries, was temporarily suspended in 1733 after he had sent the following communication to the commissioners:

> That on the 2nd instant, as he was riding at anchor in the king's barge under Ireland's Eye, Councillor Henry Coddington and his family came on board and at his request he carried him to England and landed him the 5th instant at Holyhead with 3 trunks, a portmanteau and a cloak bag with wearing apparel and a trunk with old table linen.[39]

In October 1749 Thomas Turner, surveyor, Malahide was dismissed for direct involvement with a local attorney, John Hugan, in smuggling goods from the Isle of Man.[40]

The attitude of the gentry to the revenue officers mirrored that of the commissioners to members of their staff. Officers who had been suspended and even some who had been dismissed for quite serious offences were restored on their making due submission and promising obedience for the future. The assertion of authority and the manifestation of respect for rank were regarded as important features of behaviour both inside and outside the service.

An attempt to quantify the extent of collusion with the smugglers has been made through an analysis of dismissals in the context of cessations of periods of service. Some officers included in the database were still serving at the end of 1765. Others had ceased employment in Fingal during periods for which there are no surviving minutes. However, in the case of 314 periods of service the reason for leaving is known. Table 9 summarises the position in these cases.

Dismissals formed 12 per cent of cessations. Table 10 shows their distribution by station and by reason for dismissal. It will be noted that almost half the officers dismissed were serving in Malahide. Table 11 lists the names of officers dismissed for helping the smugglers or for miscellaneous reasons which included helping the smugglers. Both Richard Sankey and Thomas Turner were later re-appointed. Sankey's case is a very strange one. He was one of the longest-serving of all the Fingal officers. He entered the service in 1714 and, apart from the short period of less than a year following his dismissal, he served until 1752, mainly at Skerries and Rush. His dismissal was based on the report of George Weston of Skerries who stated

> that he had great reason to suspect that he [Sankey] was very intimate with the runners and Mr. Leake, the gauger, [of Corduff] having informed the board that he called him in to his assistance in making a seizure, and that when he ordered him to search particular places, wherein he suspected run

> goods to be lodged, he declined it, which gave Mr. Leake cause to suspect that he was too well acquainted with the runners.[41]

On 18 June 1741 the commissioners ordered that 'Richard Sankey, late boatman at Rush, be restored the first vacancy'.[42] No reason was given for his re-appointment and one cannot help wondering if he was a double-agent.

As already mentioned, Charles Betts, Peter Dugall and William Evans were accused of being Catholic or married to Catholics as well as assisting the smugglers.[43] A particularly strange dismissal was that of the Malahide deputy surveyor, Francis Disney. In August 1764, some three years after the wholesale dismissals in Malahide, Captain Mercer reported that

> when he returned through Wales after attending his excellency, the lord lieutenant, to Chester, the Malahide barge was at Beaumaris with Henry Cotter, the smuggler, collecting his debts and that he alone had the command of her.[44]

It is hardly surprising that Disney, who was supposed to be in charge, was dismissed. If this was indeed the same Henry Cotter, who had served as a boatman in Malahide for twenty-one years until 1759 and who had leased the watch-house site to the revenue, one can understand why the station had problems. The fact that several of Cotter's children had been baptised in the Protestant church in Swords is a further indication that the smuggling fraternity was represented on both sides of the religious divide.

In contrast to the large customs station at Malahide in which officers and smugglers worked in close proximity to each other, sometimes to their mutual

Table 9. Cessation of periods of service in Fingal 1696–1765

Nature of Cessation	*No. of cases*
Absconded	4
Appointment revoked	1
Demoted	1
Died	28
Dismissed	39
Exchanged	31
Pressed into navy	1
Promoted	32
Resigned	14
Retired/charity	21
Transferred	142
TOTAL	314

Source: P.R.O., CUST 1

Table 10. Dismissals in Fingal by station and by reason for dismissal 1696–1765

Reason for dismissal	Station: Clontarf	Corduff	Finglas	Garristown	Howth	Malahide	Newhaven	Portrane	Rush	Skerries	Total
Absence from duty	1					1			1	1	4
Accepting bribes	1										1
Age and /or sickness					1						1
Assault				1		1					2
Catholic						1					1
Corruption										1	1
Debt		1								1	2
Dishonesty						2					2
Drunkenness						1	1			1	3
Embezzlement /fraud						3					3
Helping smugglers					1	3	1		1		6
Insolence						1		1		1	3
Negligence	1		1	1			1				4
Unqualified										1	1
Various causes						5					5
TOTAL	3	1	1	2	2	18	3	1	2	6	39

Source: P.R.O., CUST 1

Table 11. Fingal officers dismissed for helping smugglers 1684–1765

Name	*Grade*	*Station*	*Date of dismissal*
John Allen	Boatman	Malahide	3 March 1762
Charles Betts	Boatman	Malahide	28 January 1762
Thomas Brown	Coast officer	Newhaven	23 October 1725
Francis Christie	Boatman	Malahide	6 July 1736
Francis Disney	Deputy surveyor	Malahide	3 August 1764
Peter Dugall	Boatman	Malahide	28 January 1762
William Evans	Boatman	Malahide	28 January 1762
William Oldfield	Coast officer	Howth	4 July 1759
Richard Sankey	Boatman	Rush	14 July 1740
Thomas Turner	Surveyor	Malahide	4 October 1749

Source: P.R.O., CUST 1

profit, Garristown in west Fingal provides an interesting example of a rather isolated excise station in which a gauger had to work alone in an intensely hostile environment. This station was not formally set up until 1745. Previously the area had been serviced from Trim (County Meath).[45] Following a long correspondence with the collector at Trim the following appeared in the minutes.

> It appearing to the board that there are a great number of stills erected at Garristown in the district of Trim, which is so far from any excise officer that they can't be properly visited, by which means great frauds are committed to the prejudice of his majesty's revenue, ordered that a new gauger be appointed to take care of the said town of Garristown and that it be added to Dublin County; William Sherriff, gauger in Dublin City removed (at his request) to be gauger at Garristown, at the usual salary of £40 per annum.[46]

In 1746 the gauger reported that he had found 'eleven backs charged with pot ale in the mass house there' but, following consultation with the revenue solicitor, it was decided that there was insufficient evidence to permit their seizure.[47] As a result of complaints about frauds by private distillers the surveyor-general, and the surveyor, Langford Burleigh, were ordered to investigate the 'character and behaviour' of the gauger.[48] Following an interview with the commissioners Sherriff was dismissed for negligence.[49] Within two months his successor, Francis Drew, was dismissed for assaulting his superior, Burleigh.[50] When the next gauger, Henry Daniel, asked the commissioners to repair a house in Garristown for him the collector of Dublin county, the inspector-general of the excise and the examiner of gaugers' books submitted a joint report which stated:

> that Garristown being inhabited by a nest of clandestine distillers &c.; it has been very hurtful to the revenue that the gauger there could never

> yet be accommodated, but in one of their houses, and that, in their opinions, this expense is both justifiable and needful, regard had to the very few places in the kingdom under the same circumstances and situation, and so [it] cannot be carried into a precedent.[51]

Henry Daniel was not allowed to enjoy his house in peace for long. The following appeared in the minutes just over a year later.

> The collector of Dublin County having represented that Henry Daniel, gauger of Garristown, has been so ill-treated by the inhabitants that he is afraid to return to his duty and that that place is so lawless, that he knows of no other effectual method to bring them to an obedience of the laws, but a guard of soldiers to be quartered there for some time.[52]

In their letter to the lords justice, requesting that a sergeant and twelve men be quartered in the town for some months, the commissioners asked them to consider whether this 'may not be of service to the revenue, as well as to make the inhabitants amenable to the civil power'.

Daniel, who was unable to carry out his duties 'in the manner he ought' because of his indebtedness to the distillers was transferred in 1750.[53] He was succeeded by John Elliott. The reasons for Elliott's departure in the spring of 1753 are not known but his successor James Sterling, had no better luck than his predecessors. In April 1753, shortly after his arrival he gave an account 'of his windows having been broke by some villains, who attempted breaking into his house to intimidate him from doing his duty'.[54] Mr Caldwell, the revenue solicitor, was told to offer a reward for their discovery but there is no information about the outcome. A more serious incident occurred in 1757.[55] Burleigh and Sterling reported

> that upon an information, they found in the house of Bryan Crosbie at Garristown, seven backs of concealed pot ale with other liquors which had not paid his majesty's duty. That, while the surveyor was thus doing his duty, a mob riotously assembled in the said town who, at the said Crosbie's instigation, violently attacked him with staves and stones, by whom the said Burleigh was desperately cut and abused, and his leg broken.

Rewards were again offered and the army again called in. Sterling left Garristown a few months later. He was replaced by John Freeman but there was no improvement in the situation. In the absence of the injured Burleigh, David Moore, surveyor of excise at Limerick and pro-surveyor, Dublin County, reported in March 1758 that

> he surveyed the town of Garristown, and suspecting that John Walsh was distilling privately, by seeing a great smoke come out of his back house, he took John Freeman and George Steer, gaugers, with him, but on

> their attempting to discover the fraud, they were prevented and assaulted by several persons who threw stones at them, and put them in danger of their lives.[56]

The revenue solicitor was told to proceed against the offenders. On this occasion there was a prosecution.[57] Although the minutes for the period October 1759 to March 1760 do not survive, there is an entry in *The Public Gazetteer* for 16 October 1759 which reads:

> Friday last, found guilty at commission of oyer and terminer . . . James Barker for a riot, and assaulting Mr David Moore, one of the officers of the revenue, in the exercise of his office, fined 20 *l.* and to be imprisoned for 6 months.[58]

John Freeman had left towards the end of 1758 but the circumstances of his departure are not known as the minutes for the period October 1758 to June 1759 are also missing. The army must have been called in again as *The Dublin Gazette* reported in January 1759 that some 'revenue officers, assisted by a party of soldiers, seized a whiskey still at Garristown in the County of Dublin, which they lodged in the stores at the Custom House.[59] Freeman's successor, Joseph Macoun, died on 30 April 1760 after a little over a year's service in the station.[60] The next gauger, Charles Phipps, also found himself in difficulties. While Macoun was still alive the commissioners, on the application of the surveyor, had agreed to carry out repairs to the gauger's house.[61] After his death Macoun's widow and family refused to give up possession of the gauger's house. Macoun's widow was accused of embezzling part of the lime used for the building works and of employing the building labourers in the garden.[62] It appears that she had been drawn into the local network which was working against the revenue and she suffered a deduction from her pension as a result.

In their memorandum, which came before the commissioners on 27 April 1765, Corporal George Scott and his companions reported that they had 'lately seized under Sir Edward Newenham's command, a still at Garristown belonging to Patrick Walsh, a noted smuggler'.[63] Three days later the commissioners received a report from Newenham which read

> that he went with the army to Garristown on an information of a new still being set up in the place of the old one which was seized last week and on his arrival there he found that Charles Phipps, the gauger, had quitted Garristown, that Phipps's life is in danger from the lawless set of people who live in that town so that he is obliged to live in Balrothery although the crown pays rent for a house for the gauger there, that no gauger without a military force can do the duty and recommending that a corporal and six men be quartered there for some time &c.[64]

Once again the commissioners were obliged to write to the lords justices asking to have soldiers quartered at Garristown.

The story of Garristown is the story of the sustained and, on the whole, successful resistance of the local people to authority over a period of twenty years. The army had had to be quartered in the area four times. At least two gaugers had been forced to leave the town. Several violent incidents including serious injuries to revenue staff had occurred. Excluding gaugers still serving at the end of 1765 the average length of service in Garristown was 796 days, compared with 929 in Finglas, 1,012 in Corduff and 1,898 in Swords. The situation in Rush was rather similar and the local people there were even more successful over a much longer period. In other areas, Howth for example, outbreaks by the local people against the customs officers were more sporadic but probably just as successful.

No single pattern of behaviour prevailed throughout the region, however. The service in Skerries seems to have been relatively untouched by the infiltration of smugglers. Such accusations as there were remain unproven and may have resulted from malice. On the other hand, despite the frequent acts of violence which occurred, relations between the service and the law-breakers seem to have been extraordinarily close in certain stations, especially Malahide. The difficulties which this posed for the service are, perhaps, best summed up in the words used by the commissioners in 1759 when dismissing William Oldfield, coast officer at Howth, for refusing to name the smugglers who had killed his colleague, John Murray, whose murder he had witnessed. These killers were believed to include Nicholas Kane. The commissioners were

> also of opinion that Oldfield is induced to this conduct by being a native of Howth, bred from his youth with the said Kane, and in connection with all the persons concerned, and therefore not fit to be continued in the service.[65]

It would be difficult to find a better illustration of the conflict of loyalties to which the overlapping of the various communities in Fingal had led.

Conclusion

The story of the customs and excise service in Fingal during the period 1684–1765 is the story of a growing community. It is also the story of a community which had to survive in an increasingly hostile environment. The increase in the size of the community was not primarily due to increased population and trade, although these were, no doubt, contributory factors. It owed much more to the increasing smuggling trade, principally with the Isle of Man, and to the need for a much more energetic and sophisticated approach to guarding the coast against smugglers. Bigger and better boats, including armed vessels, were provided. The result was a very large increase in the number of low-paid boatmen needed to man the revenue barges stationed at Skerries, Malahide and Baldoyle. One of the consequences of this was the establishment of identifiable groups of relatively poor Protestants, for whom there was steady, if inadequately-paid, employment in the area. Together with the gentry and others who had arrived as a result of the changes in land-ownership after the Cromwellian and Williamite Wars they and their families formed the nucleus of small, but socially broad-based, Protestant communities. The opportunities for advancement were limited. Economically the boatmen were dependent on supplementing their meagre income by making seizures. This demanded not only co-operation with fellow-members of the crew but also good leadership by the local surveyors and their deputies. Skerries was the only area where this combination was found with any degree of consistency during the period of this study. It is perhaps significant that there was no obvious infiltration of the crew there by either the majority Catholic population or the smugglers who were numerous in the vicinity. Malahide, where the establishment was comparable in size, provides an interesting contrast. Seizures there were few. In fact, one Malahide boatman stated openly that he could get 'better bread by smuggling'. Periods of service were shorter there than in Skerries. Whereas the average length of a period of service in Malahide was less than 3½ years in Skerries it was over 5¾ years. This represented a considerable difference in the stability of the stations' personnel and it also meant that officers in Malahide had rather less time to settle down as part of the local community. Working conditions were somewhat better in Skerries. The fact that the Skerries watch-house was situated a short distance from the town meant that the crew there was rather more isolated from the smugglers than the officers in Malahide who had to work (and live) cheek by jowl with the smugglers.

Turning to external support systems the situation of the parish church close to the station seems to have been important not only in Skerries but also in other areas where this occurred. It facilitated participation by the officers in church affairs and gave them an opportunity to socialise with other members of the church community. It also permitted junior officers to take on important roles in the community, such as that of churchwarden, and several of them did so. This seems to have insulated revenue officers from any undesired interaction with their Catholic neighbours and to some degree from social intercourse with smugglers. The fact that the local gentry (the Coddingtons, principal tenants of the absentee earls of Thomond, and, later, the Hamiltons, who were resident landowners) were Protestants may also have helped. The Malahide officers had to go to their parish church in Swords, which was three miles away, to participate in vestries and few of them did so. Despite the regulations some Catholics and men married to Catholics managed to infiltrate the customs service in Malahide and both Catholic and Protestant officers worked closely with the smugglers. In that sense, at least, the customs community in Malahide seems to have been more open than that in Skerries. An attempt to summarise the nature of the overlap in the two areas has been made in Figure 12. Instances of collaboration with smugglers also occurred in other, smaller, stations.

Life was exceedingly difficult for officers in the smaller stations despite the back-up provided by the commissioners and the occasional support of the army. Violent incidents were frequently reported. Officers were often transferred for their own safety. There were many dismissals.

Overall, however, one has the impression that the men of the customs and excise service, whether serving on land or sea, were exceptionally brave. The story of their lives and exploits has not survived in the collective memory in the same way as that of their adversaries, the smugglers. Whether the Fingal experience was typical of other areas in the eighteenth century and whether the service left any longer-term legacy in the local communities are topics for exploration and investigation in the future.

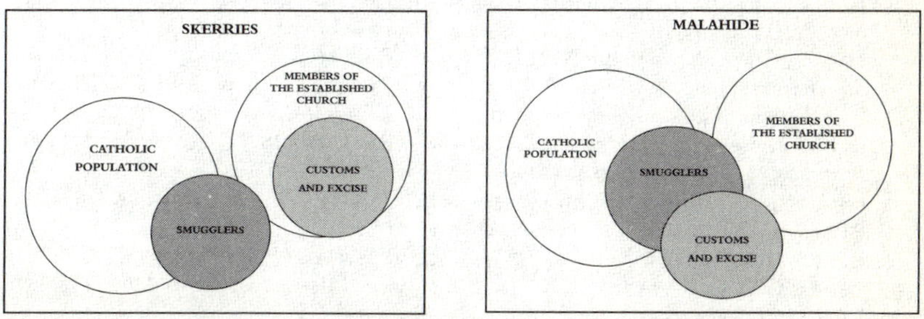

12. Overlapping communities in the eighteenth century – Skerries and Malahide

Notes

ABBREVIATIONS

Bodl.	Bodleian Library, Oxford
N. A.	National Archives, Dublin
N. L. I.	National Library of Ireland
P.R.O.	Public Record Office of England, Kew, London
Stat. Ire.	*The statutes at large, passed in the parliaments held in Ireland: from the third year of Edward the Second,* A.D. *1310, to the twenty sixth year of George the Third,* A.D. *1786 inclusive* (13 vols, Dublin, 1786)
U. C. D.	University College Dublin

INTRODUCTION

1 Alan Rogers, *Approaches to local history* (2nd ed., London, 1977), p. 4.
2 Raymond Gillespie and Gerard Moran, 'Writing local history' in Gillespie and Moran, '*A various country' essays in Mayo history* (Westport, 1987), p. 13.

THE DEVELOPMENT OF THE SERVICE IN FINGAL 1684–1765

1 14 & 15 C.II, c.9, *Stat. Ire.* (1786), ii, pp 419–493 (incl.); 14 & 15 C.II, c.8, *Stat. Ire.*(1786), ii, pp 365–418 (incl.).
2 14 & 15 C.II, c.9, paragraph XLVII, *Stat. Ire.* (1786), ii, p. 489.
3 14 & 15 C.II, c.8, paragraph XLII, *Stat. Ire.* (1786), ii, p. 382.
4 L.M. Cullen, 'The smuggling trade in Ireland in the eighteenth century', in *Proceedings of the Royal Irish Academy*, lxvii, section C, no. 5 (1969), pp 151–2.
5 P.R.O., CUST 20/62.
6 P.R.O., CUST 20/63.
7 P.R.O., CUST 20/113.
8 P.R.O., CUST 20/131.
9 Timothy Whiteing, To the right worshipful commission of his majesty's revenue in the kingdom of Ireland: a brief account of the several ports thereof in reference to the customs and imported excise. A.D. 1674, (Bodl. Rawlinson B.510, p. 1) (N.L.I., microfilm, p. 3093), ff 1 and 9.
10 P.R.O., CUST 20/56.
11 L.M. Cullen, *An economic history of Ireland since 1660*, (London, 1972), p. 54.
12 P.R.O., CUST 1/29, 27 January 1737/8.
13 P.R.O., CUST 20/106.
14 P.R.O., CUST 20/56; CUST 20/133.
15 P.R.O., CUST 1/64, 16 May 1760.
16 P.R.O., CUST 20/62.
17 P.R.O., CUST 20/69.
18 P.R.O., CUST 20/73; CUST 20/76.
19 P.R.O., CUST 20/114; CUST 1/40, 19 February 1745/6.
20 P.R.O., CUST 20/127; CUST 20/131.
21 14 & 15 C.II, c.9., Rule XLVIII, *Stat. Ire.* (1786), ii, p. 489.
22 P.R.O., CUST 1/23, 18 May 1731 and 3 November 1731.
23 17 G.II, c.7., par. II, *Stat. Ire.* (1786), vi, p. 662.
24 P.R.O., CUST 1/37, 27 July 1744.
25 19 G.II, c.4., par. IV, *Stat. Ire.* (1786), vi, p. 712.
26 21 G.II, c.4., par. VII, *Stat. Ire.* (1786), vi, p. 824.

27 23 G.II, c.3., par. III, *Stat. Ire.* (1786), vii, pp 18–19.
28 P.R.O., CUST 1/39, 6 and 16 September 1745.
29 P.R.O., CUST 1/39, 22 August 1745.
30 P.R.O., CUST 1/48, 26 April 1750.
31 P.R.O., CUST 1/18, 4 September 1725.
32 P.R.O., CUST 1/29, 25 August 1738.
33 Isaac Butler, Journal of 1744, (Armagh Public Library) (N.L.I., microfilm, p. 6486), p. 8.
34 Bernard Scalé and William Richards, *Directions for navigating into the Bay of Dublin from Wicklow Head and from Balbriggan with a particular account of the bays, roads, harbours, rocks, banks, swashes, landmarks, the setting and flowing of the tides, & c. and description of the harbours from Wicklow to Balbriggan, with a plan of each showing the depth in feet at high-water spring-tides* (Dublin, 1765), p. 26.
35 Isaac Butler, Journal of 1744, (Armagh Public Library) (N.L.I., microfilm, p. 6486), p. 2.
36 Bernard Scalé and William Richards, *Directions for navigating into the Bay of Dublin*, p. 23.
37 Isaac Butler, Journal of 1744, (Armagh Public Library) (N.L.I., microfilm, p. 6486), p. 11.
38 P. R.O. CUST 1/40, 19 February 1745/6.
39 Bernard Scalé and William Richards, *Directions for navigating into the Bay of Dublin*, p. 27.
40 P.R.O., CUST 1/17, 15 August 1723.
41 P.R.O., CUST 20/83; CUST 1/13, 7 April 1718.
42 P.R.O., CUST 1/67, 9 March 1761.
43 P.R.O., CUST 1/67, 4 April: CUST 1/69, 28 August 1761.
44 P.R.O., CUST 1/23, 12 April 1731.
45 P.R.O., CUST 1/26, 3 February 1734/5.
46 P.R.O., CUST 1/27, 2 July 1735.
47 P.R.O., CUST 1/31, 15 January 1740/1.
48 P.R.O., CUST 1/42, 14 May 1747.
49 P.R.O., CUST 1/69, 13 August 1761.
50 P.R.O., CUST 1/31, 22 January 1739/40; CUST 1/37, 2 April 1744; CUST 1/39, 26 October 1745.
51 *The Gentleman's and London Magazine*, December 1759.

WORKING FOR THE SERVICE

1 14 & 15 C.II, c.8, *Stat. Ire.* (1786), paragraph XLIII, ii, p. 383.
2 P.R.O., CUST 1/31, 10 December 1740.
3 Eileen O'Byrne (ed.), *The Convert Rolls* (Dublin, 1981), p. 226.
4 P.R.O., CUST 1/32, 29 July 1741 and 2 October 1741.
5 P.R.O., CUST 1/70, 28 January 1762.
6 P.R.O., CUST 1/89, 21 November 1765.
7 George Dames Burtchaell and Thomas Ulick Sadleir, *Alumni Dublinenses: a register of the students, graduates, professors and provosts of Trinity College in the University of Dublin* (2nd ed., Dublin, 1935).
8 P.R.O., CUST 1/75, 28 January 1763.
9 *The Dublin Journal*, 8 February 1763.
10 An essay towards the methodical collecting of his majesty's revenue of Ireland arising on the importation and exportation of goods, wherein is specified the several acts of parliament whereby they arise; the several revenues payable by them and the abatements of duty made, whether by law, compact, or for the encouragement of trade, the duty of the several officers in executing their respective employments, and the form and manner how they are to be officiated from such time as any ship appears on the coast until she be wholly unloaded, reloaded and cleared outwards ready to sail again, and the money due for her loading inwards and outwards paid into his majesty's treasury (British Library, Add. MS 4761) (N.L.I., microfilm, p. 8), f.93 ff.

An essay towards the methodical collecting of their majesties' revenue in Ireland arising on the importation and exportation of goods, wherein is named the several acts of parliament whereby they arise; the several duties payable by them and the abatements of duty made, whether by law, compact, or for the encouragement of trade, the duty of the several officers in executing their respective employments, and the form and manner how they are to be officiated from such time as any ship appears upon the coast until she be wholly unladen, reladen outwards and cleared ready to sail, and the money due for her lading inwards and outwards paid into their majesties' treasury (British Library, Add. MS 18022) (N.L.I., microfilm, p. 506), f.78 ff.

The accounts of his majesty's revenue in Ireland, from Aug. 1689 to Christmas, 1693, together with a recital by what acts of parliament each branch arises, examined by B.V. H. (Van Homrigh): with coloured plans of Kinsale, Cork, Dublin, Carrickfergus, Waterford and Londonderry (Imperfect) (British Library, Egerton MS 790) (N.L.I., microfilm, p. 1360), pp 85 ff.

11 P.R.O., CUST 1/86, 19 April 1765.
12 P.R.O., CUST 1/13, 6 June 1717 and 20 January 1717/18.
13 P.R.O., CUST 1/13, 2 September 1717; CUST 1/42, 18 April 1747.
14 P.R.O., CUST 1/16, 15 March 1721/2 and 11 April 1722.
15 P.R.O., CUST 1/14, 15 September 1719.
16 P.R.O., CUST 1/34, 9 July 1742; CUST 1/53, 14 May 1753.
17 P.R.O., CUST 1/78, 5 October 1763.
18 P.R.O., CUST 1/87, 18 and 30 July 1765.
19 John Rocque, *An actual survey of the County of Dublin, 1760* (Facsimile, Lympne Castle, Kent).
20 Bernard Scalé and William Richards, *Directions for navigating into the Bay of Dublin*, facing p. 27.
21 P.R.O., CUST 1/18, 22 October 1725.
22 P.R.O., CUST 1/24, 9 February 1731/2.
23 P.R.O., CUST 1/24, 27 April 1732.
24 P.R.O., CUST 1/26, 16 May 1734.
25 P.R.O., CUST 1/25, 8 November 1733 and 6 March 1733/4.
26 P.R.O., CUST 1/27, 26 November 1735.
27 P.R.O., CUST 1/39, 19 August 1745.
28 P.R.O., CUST 1/40, 22 March 1745/6.
29 P.R.O., CUST 1/40, 26 June and 16 July 1746.
30 P.R.O., CUST 1/41, 13 December 1746.
31 P.R.O., CUST 1/42, 26 February 1746/7.
32 P.R.O., CUST 1/42, 9 March 1746/7.
33 P.R.O., CUST 1/43, 7 January 1747/8
34 P.R.O., CUST 1/45, 3 November 1748.
35 P.R.O., CUST 1/49, 9 March 1750/51.
36 P.R.O., CUST 1/50, 22 and 29 April 1751.
37 P.R.O., CUST 1/56, 10 July 1755.
38 P.R.O., CUST 41/41, Customs Ireland, customs property, schedule of deeds, no. 17, Henry Cotter to Balthazar Cramer, p. 27.
39 P.R.O., CUST 1/40, 17 June 1746.
40 P.R.O., CUST 1/58, 13 July 1756.
41 P.R.O., CUST 1/73, 3, 8 and 18 September 1762; CUST 1/75, 19 February 1763: CUST 1/78, 26 September 1763.
42 P.R.O., CUST 1/75, 2 March 1763.
43 P.R.O., CUST 1/82, 21 July 1764 .
44 P.R.O., CUST 1/84, 22 December 1764; CUST 41/41, Customs Ireland, customs property, schedule of deeds, no. 20, Edmond Curtis to Luke Mercer, p.27.
45 P.R.O., CUST 1/89, 4 December 1765.
46 P.R.O., CUST 1/5, 27 January 1700/01.
47 British Library, Add. MS 18022 (N.L.I., microfilm, p. 506), f.79.
48 P.R.O., CUST 1/3, 4 July 1698.
49 P.R.O., CUST 1/6, 31 January 1701/2.
50 P.R.O., CUST 1/11, 30 July 1712.
51 P.R.O., CUST 1/17, 7 May 1724.
52 P.R.O., CUST 1/3, 18 November 1696.
53 P.R.O., CUST 1/5, 29 March 1701.
54 P.R.O., CUST 1/11, 31 December 1712.
55 P.R.O., CUST 1/47, 16 November 1749.
56 P.R.O., CUST 1/11, 20 July 1713.
57 P.R.O., CUST 1/29, 17 August 1738.
58 P.R.O., CUST 1/43, 17 December 1747.

59 P.R.O., CUST 1/46, 6 April 1749.
60 P.R.O., CUST 1/60, 28 July 1757.
61 British Library, Add. MS 18022 (N.L.I., microfilm, p. 506), f.80.
62 P.R.O., CUST 1/27, 2 October 1735.
63 P.R.O., CUST 1/69, 8 October 1761.
64 P.R.O., CUST 1/15, 20 August 1720.
65 P.R.O., CUST 1/38, 8 March 1744/5; CUST 1/43, 13 October 1747; CUST 1/69, 19 and 21 August 1761; CUST 1/75, 29 January 1763.
66 British Library, Add. MS 18022 (N.L.I., microfilm, p. 506), f.80.
67 P.R.O., CUST 1/16, 25 September 1722.
68 P.R.O., CUST 1/18, 9 September 1724.
69 The state of the revenue of Ireland in the year of our Lord 1693 with the ancient and present method of collecting and accounting for the several branches of it, the reasons of the change, and a view of the whole for eleven years last past. Anno 1693 (N.L.I., MS 11969), pp 21–2.
70 British Library, Egerton MS 790 (N.L.I., microfilm, p. 1360), p. 96.
71 P.R.O., CUST 1/16, 25 October 1721.
72 P.R.O., CUST 1/21, 7 March 1728/9.
73 U. C. D., Irish Folklore Department, Schools manuscript collection, 1937–8, compiled by the Irish Folklore Commission, 785, pp 95, 175 and 218; 786, p. 229; 789, pp 277 and 323.
74 Harry Bradshaw, *Folklands, 18th century smugglers of the north Dublin coast* (audio-cassette) (Dublin, 1984).
75 P.R.O., CUST 112/10, Reports by solicitor to the Irish revenue board 1744–1747.
76 P.R.O., CUST 1/39, 8 August 1745.
77 P.R.O., CUST 1/39, 2 November 1745.
78 P.R.O., CUST 1/66, 8 November 1760.
79 P.R.O., CUST 1/69, 24 September 1761.
80 P.R.O., CUST 1/69, 21 October 1761.
81 P.R.O., CUST 1/69, 11 and 17 November 1761.
82 P.R.O., CUST 1/78, 1 October 1763.
83 P.R.O., CUST 1/81, 7 April 1764; CUST 1/82, 14 July 1764.
84 P.R.O., CUST 1/86, 27 April 1765.

FAMILY FRIENDS AND THE WIDER COMMUNITY

1 Will of George Weston, P.R.O., Prerogative Court of Canterbury, October 1774, No. 382; Mrs K. Haslem, Gloucestershire County Council, County Record Office, to the author, 14 April 1998.
2 Representative Church Body Library, Holmpatrick Vestry Book, 5 October 1737, 3 October 1738, 3 October 1739, 27 September 1742 and 1 October 1760.
3 P.R.O., CUST 1/11, 11 August 1714; CUST 1/13, 12 April 1717; CUST 1/15, 4 May 1721.
4 P.R.O., CUST 1/32, 29 July and 2 October 1741.
5 P.R.O., CUST 1/70, 28 January 1762.
6 P.R.O., CUST 1/13, 8 November 1717.
7 P.R.O., CUST 1/38, 18 December 1744.
8 P.R.O., CUST 1/11/23 September 1713.
9 P.R.O., CUST 1/11, 15 October 1713.
10 P.R.O., CUST 1/16, 8 November 1722.
11 P.R.O., CUST 1/39, 6 September 1745.
12 P.R.O., CUST 20/131; CUST 1/80, 11 February 1764.
13 P.R.O., CUST 1/80, 11 February 1764.
14 P.R.O., CUST 1/75, 8 February 1763.
15 Charles Croslegh, *Descent and Alliances of Croslegh or Crossle, or Crossley of Sraitcliffe; and Coddington, of Oldbridge; and Evans, of Eyton Hall*, (London, 1904), pp 285 and 288.
16 Will of John Gay, N.A., Prerogative Will Book 1726–28; P.R.O., CUST 1/14, 28 April 1718; CUST 1/17, 6 March 1722/3 and 17 January 1723/4.
17 P.R.O., CUST 1/56, 1 October 1755.
18 J J. Digges La Touche, (ed.), *Registers of the French conformed churches of St. Patrick and St. Mary, Dublin* (Dublin 1893), p. 34.
19 Sir Bernard Burke, *A genealogical and heraldic history of the landed gentry of Great Britain and Ireland*, (London, 1894), pp 359–360; Charles Croslegh,

Descent and Alliances of Croslegh or Crossle, or Crossley of Sraitcliffe; and Coddington, of Oldbridge; and Evans, of Eyton Hall, (London, 1904), p. 288.

20 John Burke and John Bernard Burke, *A genealogical and heraldic history of the extinct and dormant baronetcies of England, Ireland and Scotland* (2nd ed., London, 1841), p. 393; Sir Bernard Burke, *Vicissitudes of families and other essays* (first series, 5th ed., London 1861), pp 156–7.

21 N.A., Sir William Betham, Genealogical Abstracts, Series V, Vol. 29(a), p. 33, no. 99.

22 Fingal Heritage Centre, Irish Genealogical Project, computer database.

23 P.R.O., CUST 1/5, 21 March 1699/1700 and 8 April 1700.

24 P.R.O., CUST 1/17, 7 May 1724.

25 P.R.O., CUST 1/19, 2 September 1726.

26 P.R.O., CUST 1/29, 25 February 1737/8.

27 P.R.O., CUST 1/35, 7 May 1743.

28 P.R.O., CUST 1/37, 19 July 1744.

29 P.R.O., CUST 1/41, 2 December 1746.

30 P.R.O., CUST 1/45, 22 October 1748.

31 P.R.O., CUST 1/75, 10 February 1763.

32 P.R.O., CUST 1/75, 2 March 1763.

33 P.R.O., CUST 1/62, 30 August 1758.

34 P.R.O., CUST 1/63, 15 August 1759.

35 P.R.O., CUST 1/26, 26 October 1734; CUST 1/32, 29 April 1741.

36 P.R.O., CUST 1/13, 16 November 1717.

37 P.R.O., CUST 1/53, 2 and 4 May 1753.

38 P.R.O., CUST 1/19, 21 March 1725/6; CUST 1/31, 10 March 1739/40.

39 P.R.O., CUST 1/25, 13 June 1733.

40 P.R.O., CUST 1/47, 4 October 1749.

41 P.R.O., CUST 1/31, 14 July 1740.

42 P.R.O., CUST 1/32, 18 June 1741.

43 P.R.O., CUST 1/70, 28 January 1762.

44 P.R.O., CUST 1/83, 3 August 1764.

45 P.R.O., CUST 1/37, 17 February 1743/4, 16 March 1743/4, 21 June and 10 July 1744; CUST 1/38, 17 and 28 September and 4 October 1744.

46 P.R.O., CUST 1/39, 3 May 1745.

47 P.R.O., CUST 1/41, 3 December 1746.

48 P.R.O., CUST 1/43, 26 November 1747.

49 P.R.O., CUST 1/44, 6 February 1747/8 and 23 May 1748.

50 P.R.O., CUST 1/45, 22 July 1748.

51 P.R.O., CUST 1/46, 10 May 1749.

52 P.R.O., CUST 1/47, 21 July 1749.

53 P.R.O., CUST 1/49, 14 August 1750.

54 P.R.O., CUST 1/53, 19 April 1753.

55 P.R.O., CUST 1/59, 8 and 10 February 1757; CUST 1/60, 28 July 1757.

56 P.R.O., CUST 1/61, 22 March 1758.

57 P.R.O., CUST 1/63, 22 September 1759.

58 *The Public Gazetteer*, 16 October 1759.

59 *The Dublin Gazette*, 13 January 1759.

60 P.R.O., CUST 1/64, 2 May 1760.

61 P.R.O., CUST 1/63, 15 August 1759.

62 P.R.O., CUST 1/69, 5 August 1761; CUST 1/70, 13 January 1762.

63 P.R.O., CUST 1/86, 27 April 1765.

64 P.R.O., CUST 1/86, 30 April 1765.

65 P.R.O., CUST 1/63, 4 July 1759.